PHILOSOPHY FOR YOUNG THINKERS

2nd Edition, Revised

Joseph Hester
Philip Fitch Vincent

Royal Fireworks Press

Unionville, New York

REVISED EDITION DEDICATED TO

Our parents
        P.F.V. and J.H.

Originally published in 1987 by Trillium Press, Inc.

Royal Fireworks Press
First Avenue, PO Box 399
Unionville, NY 10988
(845) 726-4444
FAX (845) 726-3824
email: rfpress@frontiernet.net
ISBN: 0-89824-075-1 Paperback

Printed on acid-free recycled paper by the Royal Fireworks Printing
Co. of Unionville, New York.

PHILOSOPHY FOR YOUNG THINKERS
Second Edition, Revised

Table of Contents

PART THREE: Planning and Teaching: Strategies For Implementing a Precollege Philosophy Curriculum

ACKNOWLEDGMENTS

I would like to thank Phil Vincent, Richard Stahl, and Robert Stahl for their advice, insights, and contribution in the preparation of this book. To this group of men to whom I first brought the idea of teaching philosophy to gifted students in the public schools and who shared their professional thoughts, I am indeed grateful.

To Phil Vincent, an excellent teacher of gifted students and creator of the concept of the Philosophical Inquiry Sheets, who assisted in the preparation of the Second Edition, who prepared the instructional activities for Chapters Five, Six, Seven, and Eight, and who wrote Chapter Eleven, I am more fulfilled for having been associated with him.

To Robert Stahl, I would like to express my gratitude for assisting in the overall organization of this book. Also, I would like to acknowledge Robert's insights into the area of values clarification. Robert assisted in needed modifications throughout the book.

And finally, to Richard Stahl, the person who made the writing of this book a real happening. Richard not only gave guidance and encouragement to all of the team working on this book, but it was Richard who brought the writing team together and provided the enthusiasm, organizational abilities, and ideas for completing the task.

J.H.

INTENDED USES OF THIS BOOK

The authors have prepared this book with the following uses in mind:

1. **ALL TEACHERS** will be able to use this as a basic manual with the individual activity books designed for gifted students.

2. **TEACHERS OF GIFTED STUDENTS** needing to add content and quality to their classes will be able to use this book to develop their ideas, units of study, and individual lessons in order to enrich their daily tasks.

3. **CURRICULUM PLANNERS OR SUPERVISORS** of gifted educational programs can use this book to plan, organize, and implement new and exciting educational experiences for gifted students.

4. **AN INDIVIDUAL TEACHER** wishing to add quality and dimension to old lessons can use this book to plan more effectively for both cognitive and affective lessons.

5. **CREATIVE TEACHERS** can use this book for enrichment ideas in all phases of content teaching and then build on these insights as s/he goes beyond the scope of this book.

6. **INDIVIDUAL EDUCATIONAL PROGRAMS** can be improved by following the curriculum schemes, unit goals, objectives, and plans for this book.

PREFACE

"If we do not learn from history, we shall be compelled to relive it. True; but if we do not change the future, we shall be compelled to endure it. And that could be worse."

Alvin Toffler

Many exciting and powerful ideas about working with gifted have gone unused or have been forgotten altogether because they were not translated into practical instructional materials and training activities for teachers. School Mathematics Study Group (SMSG), Inquiry training materials developed by Suchman, and Encyclopedia Britannica Foundation's (EBF) brief foray into Mathematics materials are just a few that come to mind. These innovations in creative teaching had much promise, but outside of isolated cases, they currently go unsung and unused. To challenge their abilities effectively, curriculum for the gifted must address itself to a dynamic approach involving the higher level of thinking skills. Furthermore, most educators would agree that a multidisciplinary approach for the gifted is desirable.

Yet the task of adapting present curriculum into dynamic, multi-disciplinary activities with an emphasis on higher-level thinking skills calls for a full understanding of the conditions for creative teaching and learning. *Philosophy for Young Thinkers* sets the conditions for creative teaching and learning for both the teacher and gifted students. Utilizing the vehicle of philosophy, these imaginative and well informed authors, Hester, Vincent, Stahl, and Stahl, tackle the considerable task of blending philosophical problems, thinking skills, values analysis, and activities for teachers into a dynamic whole.

The task of creating useful material for the teacher of the gifted and of helping that same teacher "retool" in philosophy is singular. A task of this nature calls for creativity, courage, commitment, and energy—all of which are reflected in this book.

The format of the book provides enough guidance to be helpful and yet enough freedom not to stifle the eager teacher of the gifted. The Philosophical Problem Sheets are a rich source of ideas and are complemented by the research findings and concepts that are translated into suggested classroom methods and instructional materials. The guidelines for K-12, divided into skills and concepts, are particularly useful in that one of the most glaring problems of current programs for the gifted is their lack of continuity and sequence.

The authors offer themselves as models of creative teaching, in that the book reflects a blending of thinking, emotions, and the freshness of first-hand experiences with gifted students in the classroom.

The chapter on planning a program provides educators the kind of help and guidance necessary to generalize principles into action. Skillfully, the reader is led to rethink and retool his/her own basic ideas on what education is all about. It will be difficult for the reader not to be actively involved as s/he deals with overarching conceptual questions such as: "What is human about humans?"

Models such as the **Hester Understanding Continuum** are also quite helpful. By using these, the reader will develop useful skills and should be able to transfer these to his/her own classroom behavior and life.

The timely concept of life-long learning is also dealt with in that the authors view the student beginning a study of facts, concepts, and skills, and embarking on a lifetime of philosophical exploration.

It will be difficult for teachers of the gifted to put this book down. It is my hope that creative use of this book will help educators realize their dream of providing appropriate challenge and education for the gifted. As the authors point out, we can no longer live for today. As life is changing so rapidly, the gifted must value and institute change in their thinking and living to create the world of the future.

Dorothy Sisk, Ph.D.
The University of South Florida

PREFACE TO THE SECOND EDITION

It has been ten years since beginning the first edition of *Philosophy For Young Thinkers*. The idea originated in our preparations for the development of North Carolina's second Governor's School Program at St. Andrews College in 1977-78. *Philosophy For Young Thinkers* was initially to be used in a six-week summer school program for high school seniors and juniors who had been selected to attend the Governor's School enrichment sessions. Since that time, much more thought and research has gone into the development of this pre-college philosophy program. By the end of 1987, a Kindergarten to Grade Nine sequentially developed curriculum will have been prepared for use in schools. In developing this program, we have tried to maintain philosophical integrity while applying the knowledge and understanding of developmental psychology to our efforts.

We are indebted to many for their advice and assistance with this program. We owe a great deal to our students with whom we first discussed our ideas and applied our methodologies. The teachers, administrators, and students of the Catawba County School District and the Wake County School District in North Carolina are fondly remembered. They allowed us to teach, try out new ideas, and evaluate our efforts in their schools. The Torrance Center at the University of Georgia is also remembered—especially Paul and Pansey Torrance—for their encouragement and assistance. The Curriculum and Instruction Department at North Carolina State University is also due our gratitude for their direction and concern for our program.

In this revised second edition of *Philosophy For Young Thinkers*, we have included many additions and changes. Chapter Three is new. It offers a fresh rationale for engaging students in higher-level thinking and philosophical problem solving. The materials for this chapter were developed in a paper read at the R.S. Hartman Institute of Formal and Applied Axiology at the University of Tennessee in 1985.

Chapter Three offers a values-centered approach to philosophy at the pre-college level. There are other approaches that a gifted curriculum can conceivably take, but we feel that students receive little exposure to a moral or ethical framework as it is. Since the Supreme Court's decision in the 1960's to ban religious exercises in the schools; the dismantling of traditional American and family values due to the rather confused decade beginning in 1965; and the emerging values-neutrality of the social sciences and guidance offices—schools have backed away from teaching a coherent set of values and traditions.

Today, schooling primarily focuses on job training and learning skills. Values teaching is looked upon with suspicion and, generally, considered an unnecessary form of indoctrination. Thus, the values which are being taught in the public schools are being filtered through two general modes of contemporary thought: cultural relativity and values neutrality. These modes support the idea that all concepts of right and wrong, political ideas, and differing forms of behavior must be tolerated as being equally valid. It is the individual alone who decides their worth.

The vacuum caused by a generation of uncertainty about teaching values and the move away from a traditional values base at home, is just now having its impact on our schools. Our answer to this social and educational dilemma is the production of a morally-centered, pre-college philosophy curriculum for gifted students. In this curriculum we shall argue for and provide a foundation for teaching such moral values as honesty, integrity, responsibility, honor, courage, and kindness. We realize that not everyone will agree with our approach. Yet, we persist, for the need has been felt.

In Part Two we have added four philosophical essays which are designed to stimulate both teacher and student. We hope that these essays will add to your insight as you prepare to teach philosophy to the youth of your school. We have added several philosophical problems to Chapter Five, the problem of free will and the problem of being born bad. Also, in Part Two, the Philosophical Problem Sheets have been completely revised along with the method of adapting these for classroom application.

Part Three is also new. Having assisted many schools with the development of gifted programs, especially those using pre-college philosophy, we thought it advantageous to share our experience with you. One of our major projects has been the establishment of a middle grades gifted program at C. H. Tuttle Middle School in the Catawba County, North Carolina School District. In Chapter Nine, we have described the basic features of this program to demonstrate how you can incorporate philosophical problem solving into your gifted program.

Chapter Ten is a revision and update of Chapter Eight of our first edition. Its purpose is to describe the Kindergarten to Grade Nine sequential pre-college philosophy program which we are now preparing for Trillium Press. Fundamentally, we have divided pre-college philosophy into three major divisions or programs:

1.   The K-3 Getting Acquainted with Philosophy Program
2.   The 4-6 Philosophical Inquiry Program
3.   The Middle Grades Philosophical Problem-Solving Program.

Each of these programs is composed of a teacher's guide and grade-level activity books. Each activity book has twenty one philosophical activities, each of which can be divided into one or more daily lessons. This chapter will also carry sample lessons from each series with ideas for teaching them.

Finally, we have added Chapter Eleven with the goal of presenting developmental issues with regard to cognitive growth and development, and cognitive moral growth and development. The research in these areas has a direct bearing on our pre-college philosophy program, the manner in which it has been written and the methodological considerations for its presentation to young people. This chapter provides the theoretical insights needed for developing a pre-college philosophy program of your own.

As we undertake this second edition of *Philosophy For Young Thinkers*, we sincerely hope that you share our excitement and enthusiasm. The renewed interest that is now being shown in education on local, state, and national levels provides a grand opportunity for us to begin using higher level thinking skills and reasoning processes with our students. The demand, the impetus, is there. It is important that we understand what is being asked of us so that we can make the proper commitments, commitments that will lead us to enrich and enhance our teaching with concepts and skills that are necessary for use in the Twenty-First Century. To you, the teacher of the gifted—and to your students—we dedicate our efforts.

PART ONE: PHILOSOPHY AT THE PRE-COLLEGE LEVEL

1

TEACHING
FOR
UNDERSTANDING

An adequate curriculum for gifted students finds its roots in the solid ground of human need in a world characterized by its quickness of change, disorganization of values, and failures in the arena of human relationships. The curriculum presented in this book encourages gifted students to chart their own course in their quest for solutions to significant human problems. But this process of integrating human knowledge and assessing human values is not an easy one. It requires a structure which promotes consistency and permits meaningful conceptualization.

THE PATH WE SEEK. . .

The curriculum model developed in this book provides an educational setting within which an impartial consideration of philosophical ideas and the evaluation of one's most deeply rooted beliefs can occur. An integration of knowledge and understanding cannot take place without direction and experience. There is a need for a plan to pool diverse information around some common theme.

This curriculum focuses on the question, ''What is human about humans?'' and seeks an integrated and comprehensive study of its many answers. Gifted students should not only be challenged to explore these answers, they should also evaluate the basic assumptions upon which they are based. The rational methods employed in this exploration have been tested in human experience and improved upon in our colleges and public schools. A study of the most important problems of human societal living cannot take place in a methodological vacuum.

This curriculum model outlines a study that will take the gifted student into the arenas of heredity and environment, the dimension of sociology, and an exploration of the descriptive dimension of being human. This curriculum moves into the prescriptive dimension of being human where the student will begin a study of the self and self-awareness, values and moral thinking, and the sources and criteria of human knowledge.

The curriculum plan proposed here is comprehensive. It integrates many kinds of knowledge. There are many philosophical problems which will be examined. Although in this one book we cannot explore all these avenues of knowledge and understanding, we can point the way, suggest a method, provide enough facts, concepts, and skills to get the student started on a lifetime of philosophical exploration. This model is merely a beginning. You—the teacher—must provide the abilities, interests, and strategies by which the task can be completed.

THE COMFORT OF OUR MINDS. . .

Change is proceeding at a pace more rapid than ever before in our society. The discoveries and innovations of the coming decades promise to make the last century appear to have progressed at a snail's pace. In the years since the end of World War II we have learned more about the universe than in all the life-spans of all the generations that went before. We have used this new knowledge to perform extraordinary feats of technology, yet there seems to be a growing awareness that knowledge alone is not enough. Rolfe Neill, Publisher of the *Charlotte Observer* newspaper, reflected:

> *As I look back at helping to rear our five children, I feel I failed them in an important area: developing the capacity to react quickly to change. I've concentrated on instilling independence and the ability to love. I left one out.*
> *Mind-baffling change seems to be the centerpiece of our time. We are slow to react because we're slow to change. We don't like it. Almost all change upsets the comfort of our mind.*
> (April 8, 1979, Page 3B)

In order to react quickly to change, one must have more than factual knowledge quickly at hand. One must also possess understanding of that knowledge. Such understanding includes:

— The appreciation of the evolution of an idea,
— The values that give meaning and significance to life, and
— An adequate methodology which expands, limits, shapes, and directs one's thoughts.

Although the mysteries of the universe are now being unlocked, there is still a great need for humankind to search for novel understandings for the best application of these new skills and knowledges.

AN UNDERSTANDING CONTINUUM. . .

The concepts of "knowledge" and "understanding" need further exploration. The word "knowledge" is usually used to refer to specific information about a subject. Thus, "knowledge" and "fact" are many times used interchangeably. Knowledge implies a "familiarity with"and "an awareness of" certain objects, ideas, people, processes, or events. Because schools and teachers have long taught factual knowledge, many of our best students have the idea that the universe is merely a pile of nouns, each distinct from the other, fragmented and isolated by the words used to refer to them.

On the other hand, "understanding" includes not only factual information, but comprehension of that information. Comprehension is more than being receptive to the facts of one's personal experiences. It is inclusive. It embodies a continuum of information and information processes.

In the biological sciences, these information processes are called "encoding." Encoding is the essential ordering process of life. Encoding includes:

— The digestion, organization, and evaluation of information,
— Information sharing which is the essential life process, and
— The patterning and duplicating of useful, life-giving information.

(See: Klapp, Orrin E. *Models of Social Order,* Palo Alto: National Press Books, 1973, pp. 20, 21.)

Encoding is inversely related to entropy. Entropy is the tendency toward disorder, randomness, and chaos in nature and within human groups. A person comprehends and uses information in order to survive. One is always struggling against nature's tendency toward randomness and disarray. Even the microscopic world shares in this process. Living cells, enzymes, and proteins take useful information from the environment which they use to continue their existence. Biologically and socially, life feeds on negative entropy. Encoding is life-sustaining.

For human beings, comprehension or understanding is the matrix of encoding. It includes the organization of facts, concepts and values via the rational process. Thus, encoding allows humans to live at more than rudimen-

tary levels. It accounts for one's particular conception of the world. One's willingness and ability to share this storehouse of digested information is the process by which individuals restore themselves and maintain active human relationships. One's ability to act upon these resources includes:
— Communication,
— Social adjustment,
— Negotiation,
— Reciprocation, and
— Culture building.

One's ability to create order and balance within human societies includes:

1.   Gathering and describing the data of raw experience, which includes confronting the "that which is" of one's experience.

2.   Forming concepts, which is the ability to group experiences under broad and general mental categories. This level includes gathering factual information and organizing this information according to particular cause-and-effect relationships.

3.   Value development, which begins with the appraisal of the facts and concepts relative to one's biological and sociological environments that give meaning, usefulness, and significance to one's life.

4.   Rational organization, which gives order to one's experiences. Reason functions to organize and validate the concepts and values included in a person's unique way of life.

Taken all together, these four learning modalities complete an understanding continuum around which one can arrange both the learning and behavioral objectives of day-to-day teaching. From this point of view, the teaching process should include the following learning behaviors:
— Gathering relevant factual information,
— Investigating the concepts suggested by such data,
— Evaluating pertinent attitudes and behaviors, and
— Organizing this process through the utilization of necessary critical thinking skills.

Figure One will help you organize these four levels of learning and teaching for practical application in the classroom.

THE HESTER UNDERSTANDING CONTINUUM

Level One: **Factual Knowledge**
                              (''that which is'')

- -

Level Two: **Concept Formation**
                              (mental organization)

- -

Level Three: **Value Development**
                              (appraisal/evaluation)

- -

Level Four: **Rational Organization**
                              (explanation/consistency)

FIGURE 1

From Level One to Level Four, each subsequent level includes all previous levels. When a person learns according to this methodology, it is understood that that person's behaviors are founded on both KNOWLEDGE and UNDERSTANDING. The final test of this process lies with the survival chances it provides for the human species.

One may wish to argue that the survival chances of an individual or group of individuals—such as a society or culture, family or educational institution—is relative to the efficiency of the methods it uses to satisfy its survival needs. The contention of this book is that consistently following the method outlined in Figure One will produce more information and understanding.

EDUCATING FOR THE FUTURE. . .

Educational leaders recognize that an individual cannot foresee exactly which knowledges, concepts, values, or skills will be needed for future living. No one knows exactly what path the future will take. Thus, IF gifted students are to have understandings as well as knowledges which allow for flexibility and growth, THEN it is imperative to ensure that they will receive the studies they need.

There is a growing need for:

1.   The development of attitudes and abilities that will help gifted students when confronted with difficult challenges, both educational and social;

2.   The discovery of better and more creative solutions to urgent problems;

3.   The retention of intellectual and emotional flexibility; and,

4.   The maintenance of a universal and unbiased vision of people and their role in one's future course of action.

A major purpose for developing this program is to explore with our gifted students an integrated and multidisciplinary study of humankind that will enable them to enrich their personal understanding of what it means to be human. This program is designed to bridge the gap between the sciences and humanities, and to explore the major questions that continue to plague inquiring minds. Any culturally-tested understanding or any pertinent information cannot be consciously omitted from this program. The intention is to help the gifted student create a unified picture of the human species evolving through time within the natural environment. If these students are able to discover their own personal role in this process, then they will be able to view the human situation with greater self-involvement and wider perspective.

The curriculum for gifted students presented in this book has five distinguishing characteristics:

1.   It is an integrated and comprehensive study;

2.   It explores concepts and values, thinking processes and facts;

3. It is concerned with human physical and social development in the past, present, and future;

4. It suggests self-understanding as a prerequisite to one's becoming aware of personal beliefs, individual biases, and philosophical commitments; and,

5. It offers no dogmas or prescriptions to follow except one: the rational exploration of the fundamental physical, social, and subjective dimensions of human involvement.

THINKING SKILLS...

As most teachers are aware, teaching the "three r's" has always been the backbone of public education in America. Subject matter is mandated by prescribed educational curricula. More often than not, the very best students are left unchallenged by teaching that is directed to the average intellect, which is more interested in the mechanical and factual than in ideas and values, and tuned to the uncommitted and middle-of-the-road position..These students, who probably will be active in shaping the future, have little time in their academic hours for concentrated attention on the most basic and widely used set of cognitive skills: **THINKING**.

A comprehensive program for the gifted should assist them in becoming independent thinkers. Inquiry skills development can provide a means whereby the gifted student is able to separate truth from falsehood, identify and analyze difficult problems, and develop criteria for evaluating the solutions offered for these problems. The inquiry approach has the additional benefit of encouraging these students to take responsibility for their own capacities for discovering, creating, and assessing meaning in the workday world.

The **INQUIRY METHOD** is one in which the student is able to:

1. Recognize a problem which is posed in the classroom environment;
2. Formulate a tentative solution or hypothesis to the problem;
3. Acquire the appropriate information for solving the problem;
4. Analyze, evaluate, and interpret this body of information;
5. Explore the sources and logical connections or relationships;
6. Explain these connections or relationships;
7. Test the hypothesis by using newly acquired information;

8.   Modify the hypothesis if necessary and restate it as a generalization; and
9.   Use this hypothesis to account for other, similar situations.

Inquiry is essentially a scientific operation. Students must be called upon to master this process. Then and only then will they have a disciplined method of approaching the important questions that are now haunting contemporary society. These students will possess better equipment to learn independently in a world where human knowledge increases daily.

Another important benefit of mastering thinking skills is the ability to review thoughtfully the fundamental assumptions that underlie the social and scientific institutions of today's world. Teaching for thinking and understanding as well as for epistemic facticity may help to loosen the shackles of closed thinking that have plagued the American educational system for so many years. For this purpose, the teacher must possess the ability to identify the various components of societal and personal living for either propagation or rejection and to lead in their rational and value-centered appraisal.

THE PHILOSOPHICAL MEDIUM...

An adequate program for the enrichment of gifted students includes at least three basic ingredients:

— An expansion of self-awareness,
— The development of rational methods, and
— An adequate medium for the expansion and deepening of their ideas and values.

The medium used in this curriculum has long been neglected in the public schools. Most of our educational time has been devoted to the acquisition of knowledge. It is the contention of this book that **PHILOSOPHY** will be a positive aid for students as they seek new understandings about the human situation; and they will be able to incorporate these understandings into their own societal strivings.

Chapter Two will explain the direction of this philosophical curriculum in more detail. Also, it will provide a definition of the discipline of Philosophy which will be useful as this curriculum unfolds and the problems addressed by it are explored.

2 PHILOSOPHICALLY SPEAKING

"DARE TO KNOW"

In 1784 Immanuel Kant defined the Eighteenth Century Enlightenment as humanity's emergence from its self-imposed tutelage, and gave it the motto SAPERE AUDE: "Dare to Know." The motto was Kant's challenge to his contemporaries to take the risk of discovery, exercise the right of unfettered criticism, and seek a broader base of understanding and meaning.

As in Kant's motto, the intention of the curriculum model presented in this book is to challenge gifted students to understand themselves: to explore diligently and patiently the natural, ideological, and mythological past from which they have emerged; to discover the many determinants of their behaviors; to put their most precious beliefs to the fire of critical and unfettered thinking; and then, to choose patterns from which they can mold their future existence.

The task of this curriculum is philosophical, but it tries to avoid the contemporary "squint" which affects much of today's professional philosophizing. This curriculum will include a multidisciplinary approach to the study of humankind and will endeavor to develop a synthesis between the descriptive and prescriptive studies of the **HUMAN BEING** and **BEING HUMAN**.

Fundamentally, the curriculum presented here begins with the exploration of the question, "What is human about humans?" The curriculum will encompass both the natural and the socio-cultural histories of humans. Also, it will inquire into the nature and activities of the self, the problems associated with developing and assessing a usable moral frame of reference, and the sources, criteria, and scope of knowledge.

The purpose of this curriculum is to assist the gifted student in discovering his/her own personal role in the philosophical process. This plunge into the unknown and unused regions of the mind will help him/her view the world with greater depth and a deeper sense of self-involvement. In addition, it will nurture individuality by providing him/her with a different language and a different mode of thinking, and will help each reach creative potentials and make critical decisions. The expansion of mind, the desire to probe into one's most delicate beliefs, and the willingness to take the risk of reconsidering these ideas can be a most exciting adventure.

PHILOSOPHY AS RE-THINKING. . .

Philosophy, originally "the love of wisdom," is first a **RE-THINKING OPERATION**. This concept needs to be emphasized. Even in the physical and human sciences, the fundamental principle of objectivity is that of re-thinking or reconsideration. That is, to be objective one ought to be willing to reconsider the underlying beliefs and common sense assumptions which support the behaviors indigenous to his/her way of life. If a truth-seeker is unwilling to rethink the raw data of experience or the sources of such data when fresh information is discovered, then there can be no basis for comparison when conflicts and inconsistencies occur.

When an individual engages in the activity of values clarification, the values which are held near and dear must undergo rational scrutiny. When engaged in scientific research, each fact and every theory must be subjected to scientific verification. Then and only then can one consider those facts and theories to be objective in the scientific sense. Even the methodology of scientific verification must, sooner or later, come under the critical eye of reconsideration.

If a person is unwilling to reconsider these beliefs, theories, or values in the ongoing context of human usage, then their objective status will be greatly diminished and their pragmatic value severely impaired. The process of reconsideration can be utilized to keep one's thoughts and methods free from dogmatic assumptions and biased actions.

One of the major functions of education is to develop in students the ability to think clearly and consistently about difficult problems. The philosophical life is reflective of this quality. No matter what age the person, the habit of thinking as opposed to simply acting on impulse or letting the mind wander as it will during inactive moments is evidence that that person has taken up the philosophical life.

If there is a universal bond among those who engage in philosophical inquiry, it is surely the **DESIRE TO KNOW**. Imagination and curiosity, seemingly natural dispositions in younger children, ought to be promoted throughout one's life. In working with middle school and high school gifted students, it has been discovered that for many this passion for knowing is now only a flickering light.

— What has happened to these students?
— What has happened to our teaching methodologies?
— Is that light lit dim in us as well?

As teachers consistently apply thinking and re-thinking operations in their classroom procedures and develop a student-centered classroom environment which is intellectually flexible and focuses on question-asking procedures, the student will:

1. Be able to identify and transmit a body of understandable information;

2. Gain an understanding of important concepts and generalizations when facts are organized in meaningful ways;

3. Develop constructive values and attitudes toward learning and toward people as success in problem-solving skills is achieved; and

4. Become more successful in developing context-related skills in science, math, language arts, and social studies.

By utilizing The Hester Understanding Continuum (Figure One) developed in the Introduction of this book, the teacher can plan better for these behaviors and thinking skills. If the curriculum presented in this book is to become comprehensive and integrated, then each of these understanding and thinking areas must be planned for and developed. The teacher's role in this process is that of curriculum facilitator. The teacher should suggest problems for analysis, provide resources, facilitate processes, and help each student test the validity of the ideas and concepts generated. In this way, the gifted student's education will be more than auxiliary to his/her life experiences; education will add needed depth and meaning to the student's life.

PHILOSOPHY AS CONCEPT-SEEKING. . .

Fundamentally, philosophy is concept-seeking. Concepts are more general than facts. They refer to one's conceptualization of a class of objects or events. Thus, concepts are mental constructs (one's mental filing system) which isolate from experience the common attributes which identify the facts of one's experiences. Examples of concepts are "equality," "triangle," "nation," "animal." An individual harvests these from the facts of raw experience. They are natural abstractions that are used to explain new experiences and give commonality to old ones. Einstein believed that the invention of concepts and the building of theories upon them was one of the great creative properties of the human mind.

From the classroom lecture to the standardized achievement test, many of the educational experiences of gifted students are oriented to gathering, describing, and recalling facts. Very little time is given to concept-seeking. But facts are forever changing. For example, in Africa many new nations have arisen in the past twenty-five years. It took only a single war to change the map of Europe in the 1940's. But the concept of "nation" has remained virtually unaltered. Some concepts are stable.

A curriculum based on concept-seeking will be more insightful, inclusive, and enriching than one which is oriented only to the gathering and dissemination of facts.

Concepts have the following characteristics:

1.   They are based on habitual paths of association, the cataloging and categorizing of information into mental patterns;

2.   They are mentally constructed and, therefore, are categorically different from either sensing or imagining, yet have properties of each;

3.   They are inclusive in that many different but similar facts can be filed under a single concept;

4.   They possess stability and, therefore, have explanatory value, and

5.   They are the basis of explanatory procedures: the cause-and-effect sequence of past experience.

PHILOSOPHY AS ASSESSING BASIC ASSUMPTIONS. . .

So often one's answers to the question, "What is human about humans?" will involve elements of both the cognitive and affective dimensions of human experience. On some occasions a person can be unaware that these two areas have been blended into a unified conception of what s/he considers human life to be. When this occurs, some of a person's pronouncements about human nature, values, knowledge, or the self will be left unsupported.

To illustrate this situation, consider the following questions:

1.   Is human nature fundamentally good, bad, or neutral?

2.   Is human behavior the result of free will or is it almost completely determined by biological forces, the social environment, or a supernatural being?

3.   Do human beings and animals behave according to the same laws or are there basic differences between animal and human nature?

4.   What ought to be done to improve the future of human beings?

Each of these questions is involved in answering the more general question, "What is human about humans?" Before reading further in this book, complete the following exercise.

— Answer the above four questions without referring to sources beyond your own mental capacities.
— Next, pick out the factual components of your answers.
— Then pick out the affective or emotional parts of your answers.
— Then, pick out the affective or emotional parts of your answers.
— Now, which component, the factual or affective, is more reliable?
— Do you have good reasons for your answers?
— Are your facts supported by evidence, logically consistent?
— Why did you choose some facts and not others?
— When you have finished the above, rewrite your answers in the light of any new information or ideas.

As you are now aware, your answers to these questions reveal the essence of your traditional beliefs and deeply rooted assumptions. These beliefs and assumptions are saturated with your cultural and biological past. They support, either strongly or weakly, your philosophical point of view. Such a point of view structures the body of information by which one is apt to analyze, catalogue, and evaluate the components of her/his sociocentric universe. These answers also determine what one believes about things, events, ideas, and behaviors; or how one probably will act in certain circumstances.

There is a need for the teachers of the gifted to re-examine these assumptions and beliefs. One's effectiveness in facilitating such a re-examination among his/her students is based on how much one is willing to complete this needed task for himself or herself.

Consider the following argument:

1.   The concepts contained within a person's philosophical point of view act to shape one's attitudes and dispositions toward different people and events.

2.   One's attitudes are predispositions to one's actions.

3.   Thus, one's actions are rooted in either examined or unexamined assumptions.

One's philosophical points of view are alive with concepts, beliefs, assumptions, and the attitudes which change them into actions. Such is the mode of internal understanding. This will be reflected in the answers given to the four questions above.

The task is clear. The responsibility is ours. We who teach gifted students must re-examine our own assumptions before we give this task to our very best students. This task of re-evaluation is essential to and prerequisite to an adequate application of the curriculum model presented in the next chapter.

There are no easy answers—just tough questions. Some of your answers will remain tentative and inconclusive. Others will be set aside for future exploration. The pleasure and pain of it is a crucial part of the reflective lifestyle. Your task has only just begun.

Remember: Education is not just information gathering and data processing, learning a new skill or passing a normed test of basic skills. Education is also discovery, and discovery always occurs on the personal level. No one can discover how free you are or find purpose in your life. Someone else's purpose might be your hangup and vice versa.

If Socrates was correct when he uttered the words: "The unexamined life is not worth living," then the curriculum in the next chapters challenges teachers and gifted students to enter the process of assessing the basic assumptions of their lives, to make life worth living.

PHILOSOPHY: A VALUES-CENTERED APPROACH

To philosophize is to wonder about life—
about right and wrong,
love and loneliness,
war and death,
about freedom, truth, beauty, time . . .
and a thousand other things.
                                        James L. Christian

PHILOSOPHICAL RESPONSIBILITY . . .

Since 1977 we have worked toward the development of a pre-college
philosophy curriculum which seeks an understanding of philosophical problems, endeavors to develop reasoning skills in our young people, and focuses
upon studies in ethics, epistemology, and metaphysics as legitimate concerns
of the public school curriculum. The reasoning abilities which we have
selected to emphasize in this curriculum are critical thinking, research, and
creative problem-solving.

Conceptually, this curriculum pursues an understanding of the many answers to the question, "WHAT IS HUMAN ABOUT HUMANS?" It can
be used in connection with almost any subject area and offers a sequentially
organized K-12 package of cognitive skills and affective concepts.

In 1983 the first materials related to this philosophy curriculum were
published under the title *Philosophy For Young Thinkers*. Now we are in
our second edition. In this book the promise and peril of a philosophical
education for our young people is discussed. Also, in it is suggested curricula
strategies, unit outlines, and learning activities for teaching philosophy to
young people. In 1984, a companion volume of activities was published
under the title *Cartoons for Thinking*. This book utilizes political cartoons
to teach problems in social and moral philosophy, critical thinking, and
problem-solving. In 1985 another interesting volume in this series was published, *Computer Ethics*, which takes a serious look at the various ethical
issues surrounding the use or misuse of the computer. In 1987-1988 a detailed

set of materials for teachers and students in the primary grades through the middle grades will be published. The purpose of these materials is to extend this program throughout each grade level in the public school curriculum.

The impetus for this work comes from many sources but primarily from the belief that, as the 20th Century draws to a close, we are losing the battle of the quest for the "possible human." Today we are witnessing the collapse of many of our elementary moral connections (our moral bridges to the future). An analogy may prove beneficial:

> On June 28, 1983, the Mianus River Bridge collapsed on Interstate 95 in Connecticut with fatal results. Since then, much has been made of the issue of this nation's deteriorating stock of bridges. Out of all the clamor has arisen a common realization: that Americans seem happier building new bridges than maintaining the ones they already have.

The point is quite clear: possibly like those who have failed to maintain America's bridges, we too have failed to maintain the moral connections which bind humans, human institutions, and our natural environment together. We have become a nation that prefers to throw away its used appliances, outdated automobiles, marriages, old persons, children—its moral connections—and with them the spirit and idealism of our democratic foundations.

Why do we shy away from human maintenance? Why do we have such a heady concern for the new? What did the collapse of the Mianus River Bridge tell us about ourselves, our motives, our goals?

The sad truth is that we have become a nation of "chuckers-out." We have taught our children to avoid critical thinking and, in doing so, have wrapped them in an insulated cocoon of escapist movies, television soap operas, and public school text books that fail to challenge the most simple-minded student. We have made little effort to expose our children to fundamental human values and moral dilemmas. Also, we have failed to teach them even the rudiments of critical reflection which allows them to appraise the value of an idea, a social convention, or a moral principle.

Well, so what? Why not move on? Why not scrap the old and go for the new?

Fair enough, as long as newness is not a mere novelty and as long as we creatively maintain the things most precious to us. But here, especially, the evidence should give us pause. An increasing divorce rate suggests that we are hard pressed to maintain our marriages. An employment pattern showing workers drifting in and out of jobs suggests that we are giving too little thought to maintaining careers. Even the care of the elderly, the maintenance of the dignity of maturity, may be slipping from family responsibility into institutional control.

Are we doomed to expire in a frenzy of novelty? Hardly! The growth of preservationist groups speaks to our yearning to restore, recycle, and to renovate. So does our pregnant awareness of the challenges revolving around marriage, careers, aging—and bridges. **Yes, we are capable of creative maintenance!**

But to some "creative maintenance" may sound paradoxical; and so it is—unless we understand that creativity entails a useful channeling of spontaneity, and that maintenance implies a nurturing of the patterns and institutions which permit all this channeling to take place.

Seen in this way, maintenance itself becomes an art. It also becomes a commitment to support the projects of an earlier age, a trust that newness will be fostered, not undercut, by respect for the intelligent foresight of past builders. Some of them built bridges, some marriages, others built careers, and some built a lifetime of maturity. Our task has been, for a number of years, to assist in the construction of moral connectives (bridges) to the future. Our children are in need of moral maintenance. The more we make a priority of creative maintenance, the more we have discovered that our past builders laid an adequate foundation. The responsibility is ours and we must make sure that these bridges are taken care of, that they do not become weaker from nonuse and misuse.

Creative maintenance entails the necessity of developing the skill of self-generative learning in each student. This need grows more obvious and urgent each day. The incredible and accelerating explosion of knowledge, coupled with the frighteningly complex social, political, and economic problems of our contemporary era, demand an educational process that produces active, autonomous, self-generative learners. Productive individuals in the contemporary world must have the emotional stability to confront continuous change and the necessary skills to engage in a continuous process of personal and group problem solving.

As Educators, the time has come for us to ask—not what kind of education we desire to provide for our young people, but what kind of human being we want to emerge from our efforts at schooling them. What would we have 21st Century Man be? A partial answer to this question just might be that because we live in a society which affirms the basic values of democracy (values such as openness, freedom, and equality); we should first see to it that, in our schools, social and cultural indoctrination is accompanied by the teaching of critical reflection and independent judgment. Thus, as a young person achieves greater maturity, s/he will be able to assess the validity of the beliefs and habits in which s/he has been nurtured. In this way, s/he will be better prepared for nurturing the old as well as for creating new pathways to the future.

In 1951, Edgar S. Brightman gave to us these insights:

> *As the second half of the 20th Century opens, freedom, reason, the rights of man, the worship of God, the love of truth, beauty, and goodness—all of man's highest values— are threatened by 'military necessity,' the totalitarian state, materialistic theories and practices, and ruthless competition.*
>
> *A conflict of ideals is raging in the world. It is not merely a conflict between East and West, or between science and tradition, or between communism and capitalism, or between political and economic democracy, or even between totalitarianism and freedom. It is a struggle 'in the minds of men' about ultimate values.*
>
> Edgar S. Brightman
> *An Introduction To Philosophy*

We hope that the curriculum in pre-college philosophy which we are now preparing will, in some way, contribute to the moral maintenance of our most precious resource—our young people. As we seek new ways to engage children in discussing and writing about significant human problems, the ethical overtones are obvious; but one should remember that it is impossible to enhance the morality of a generation of young people without also changing how they think. Critical thinking and the development of reasoning processes must become a way of life for our children.

In 1984, speaking at the University of North Carolina at Charlotte, Richard Ekman, from the National Endowment for the Humanities, remarked that, "Too few [of our students] are concerned with the uses of language, with ethics and critical thinking, with parallels between the present and the past, or with ideas that help them define and understand their culture."

So, the challenge is ours. Maybe, just maybe, we in philosophy, the humanities, and education will not deny our mission. So much is at stake in our world today.

In his book, *Philosophy: An Introduction to the Art of Wondering*, James L. Christian tells us that "...in this tribal world, someone must still keep watch. He must stand apart, as best he can, to try to keep life in perspective. The party members won't do it, nor will the fearful, the brainwashed, the prejudiced, or the bigoted. But there must be someone.'' Our primary goal in developing this book and its following series of activities and teachers' guides is to assist students in staying close to all the realities as possible; to help them with their struggle against being manipulated and polarized; to help them to develop their cognitive abilities and affective sensitivities so that each may reach moments of greater clarity and perspective. As Christian reflects: "There must be someone who remains sensitively aware of the essential humanness in every position that human beings take.''

Teaching philosophical concepts and critical analysis to young people is a demanding task and a never-ending venture. There is a deep feeling of satisfaction to watch young people grow and mature both intellectually and morally. A teacher feels this in even a deeper way when these young people are able to discover success at higher levels of achievement. An education that fails to come to grips with the fundamental questions of human-living is an inadequate education. Life changes. About this fact we need be aware. There are few answers that are able to satisfy everyone and most answers, like life itself, cannot be answered with any finality. The basic questions that human beings ask themselves call for detailed analysis, the application of problem-solving, and careful evaluation. The quest is life-long.

Piaget talks about the importance of producing autonomous students. Autonomy implies independence, thus the importance of students who are able to think for themselves. The creation of moral autonomy in our students demands that our classrooms are places of discussion and discovery. It demands that critical thinking and moral evaluation are not only taught, but that students are given the freedom to exercise the skills and ideas which they have learned. Piaget tells us that classrooms organized around rewards and punishments or the teacher as an absolute authority will not have these results.

Thus, if we are to achieve excellence in our teaching, we need to commit ourselves to those educational principles which are certainly basic in a thriving democratic state. Stale, closed-minded thinking is certainly contrary to those methods which are able to produce autonomous, independently minded young thinkers. A sense of purpose and direction in these matters will motivate us to develop lessons which promote these skills.

The development of habits of intellectual inquiry, high standards of moral integrity, a willingness to examine all the information available to us, and a devotion to truth are essential as our young people begin their transition into adulthood. A decade ago, in the beginning stages of this pre-college philosophy program, we made these commitments. We sincerely hope that you too catch the spirit which has infected us and the vision which we also share for our young people.

An Example May Work . . .

Colman McCarthy, a columnist for the *Washington Post*, tells the story of taking four teenagers to see the recent movie "Platoon." What these teenagers did not know was that the average age for the Vietnam soldier was nineteen. On the way to the theater, the teenagers were lighthearted, joking, and ribbing. McCarthy reflects that they had seen "Rambo," "Top Gun," and "Heartbreak Ridge," all which glorified war and "went well with popcorn and the corn of pseudo-patriotism."

Although the story called "Platoon" is billed as a story about the Vietnam War, it's really about teenagers. It depicts a diverse group of young men exiled for a year in Vietnam. As McCarthy says, "They get lost in jungles and soon, in the unvaryingness of military violence, they lose moral direction. Members of the platoon kill women, bash the brains of children, set a village afire and murder each other. They are Americans."

After returning home from the movie, McCarthy asked the teenagers some questions about the movie. One question asked which scene made the strongest impression on them. One of the boys in the group thought that it was where an American soldier shot a poor helpless woman in the head and then his insensitivity of taking a little girl and holding the gun to her head, threatening to kill her if the old man didn't stop crying over his wife's death. The boy remarked: "Before I saw this, I was led to believe that we were the good guys, and the Vietnamese were the cruel and insensitive ones."

The teenagers were asked what the moral of the film was. They wrote:

"To show a movie on facts, not heroism, glory or how glamorous war is."

"The moral? How futile the whole thing was since at the bottom of it, like the movie says, they were fighting themselves and not the enemy. Therefore it shows a problem with society—a society which cannot come to terms with itself and which must therefore find an alternative."

"There isn't any (moral). . . . The film is just a very moving depiction of the Vietnam War."

"War is hell. The struggle of war is horrible and in this particular incident almost pointless or accomplishing almost nothing."

After questioning these teenagers, McCarthy wondered if he had been right in taking these young people to see this kind of starkness. He reflected:

After reading their answers to my questions, why not? Through other films, their souls had already been exposed to the contamination of the war cult. "Platoon" was an antibody. Through it, health might be restored: the health of clearheadedness that the young will need when adults issue the next war call.

The purpose of our centering this philosophy curriculum on ethical issues and concepts is quite clear: we not only wish to assist in the development of the rational health of the young people of America, but their moral health as well. We really cannot separate the two. In the final chapter of this book we speak about the cognitive moral development of young people. It is pointed out that youngsters cannot reason at the higher levels of moral development unless first they can reason at all. Cognitive morality depends upon the development of the ability to reason, to think clearly and logically about important human issues. You will note in our essay concerning "Moral Objectivity," that one of the three basic commitments one must make to reason morally is a commitment to reason, to consistent and reconsidered thought about our basic ideas, concepts, and beliefs.

Our task with young students is explanation and understanding. Ethical truths will not be found within the contemporary scientific picture. No ethical truths are established in any scientific theory or tested by any scientific procedure. The instruments of science and technology reveal no ethical facts. Thus, if there are ethical facts, what kind of facts are these, what makes them hold true? This is what we want to discover. This is what we want to discuss with young people.

Our various questions will come from one: how are we valuable and precious? The answer to this question will reveal to us the answers to other questions such as, "Does life have meaning?", "Are there objective ethical truths?", "Do we have free will?" and "What is the nature of our identity as selves?"

These various questions arise from, are shaped and made vivid by, a concern with our value, significance, importance, stature, and preciousness. That is, if our lives cannot have meaning, if we have no worth that the actions of others ought to respect, then we are devoid of value.

In the essays which we have included in Part Two, we wish to reach the conclusion that we are worthwhile and precious. Although others may reach a different conclusion about humanity's worth and significance, our philosophical goal is getting to the place worth being, even though the investigation may change and deepen the idea of worth. There is no scientific or logical law which says that we must stop our philosophical reasoning short of our objectives and goals. The door of reason will stay open until our goal has been reached.

Of course no philosophical inquiry, with a foregone conclusion, can restrict itself to the central questions; in pursuing these, we are always led to others as well. That we aim our philosophy at a conclusion, does not guarantee it will be reached. Yet, our curriculum model suggests common themes and in their pursuit we are led to others as well. As we permit the linkages to emerge, they will form conceptual connections to strengthen the whole, as a framework.

Even though we have designed this curriculum with a definite purpose, our task is not coercive. Philosophical training molds arguers; it trains students to produce arguments and to criticize and evaluate them. A philosopher's seriousness is judged by the quality of his or her arguments. Just because philosophy and its arguments are powerful, the terminology of the philosophical art appears coercive. A philosophical argument is an attempt to get someone to believe something, whether he or she wants to believe it or not. Yet, if we respect other persons and value them as we value ourselves, we should aim our curriculum at elaboration, explanation, and understanding rather than coercion. The valuable person cannot be fashioned by committing philosophy upon him.

A motive in developing this curriculum is to stimulate new thoughts and deepen and extend these thoughts in order to enrich the persons whom we are teaching. At no point is the student forced to accept anything. He or she is permitted to move along gently, exploring personal thoughts and the ideas which are being openly discussed and about which he or she is reading. The students explore together with the teacher and the reading materials, moving only where and when they are ready to. Another motivation for this curriculum is puzzlement, curiosity, a desire to understand and not a desire to produce uniformity of belief. The philosophical goal of explanation and understanding rather than proof is more consistent with the goals of reasoning and cognitive moral development. It is our goal.

The ideas in this book are set forth in a very tentative spirit; not only do we not ask you to believe they are correct, we do not think it important for us to believe that they are correct, either. Still, we believe, and hope that you will find it so, that this curriculum (explanations) are illuminating and worth considering, even worth teaching to others. Also, that the process of seeking and elaborating explanations, being open to new possibilities, new wonderings and wanderings, free exploration, is itself a delightful undertaking. Can any pleasure compare to that of wondering about or explaining a new idea, a new question?

PART TWO:
A
MULTIDISCIPLINARY
CURRICULUM FOR
GIFTED EDUCATION

4 A CURRICULUM MODEL FOR INVESTIGATING HUMANNESS

CHAPTER

MODEL ANALYSIS. . .

The purpose of this chapter is to help provide some answers to the question, "What is human about humans?" The answers proposed to this question will compel the student to re-think many of his/her basic beliefs and favorite theories about human life. To answer this question more thoroughly one needs to approach it through a variety of subjects and interrelated knowledges. After all, the basic advances in scientific knowledge often spring from the cross-fertilization of knowledge from different specialties. A multi-disciplinary approach to the study of "humankind" will provide the student with the background to evaluate the answers to this, the most fundamental of questions.

There are two sides to the question, "What is human about humans?" One is the descriptive side. Here, the student will be interested in the factual answers given by the biological and sociological sciences. The other is the prescriptive side which takes as its purpose the evaluation of the nature of being human. Although the methods used on either side of this study will be based on scientific and logical procedures, the subject matter will be somewhat different. The descriptive dimension is interested in the facts that have set in motion the emergence of human life. The prescriptive dimension is fundamentally evaluational and will suggest ways to improve self-esteem, one's personal and societal values, and one's methods of gathering, organizing, and disseminating knowledge.

A curriculum for investigating answers to the question, "What is human about humans?" should contain the various components just described. Figure Two provides a curriculum model which incorporates the key ingredients needed in such an investigation. This Chapter and Chapters Five through Eight will help expand this model to make it a practical tool for teachers to use in planning and implementing gifted programs.

The strategies for carrying this curriculum model into effective classroom activities relate to the teacher's ability to design and implement inquiry lessons. An inquiry lesson is an instructional means that allows students the flexibility to generate and test their own ideas about what they believe to be true, real, and of value. In inquiry, the PROCESS of learning is just as important as what is learned. The emphasis is on concept development. There is no stoppage of ideas. The teacher's role in this process is to suggest problems, provide resources and, generally, help with the development and testing of ideas.

"What is Human About Humans?"

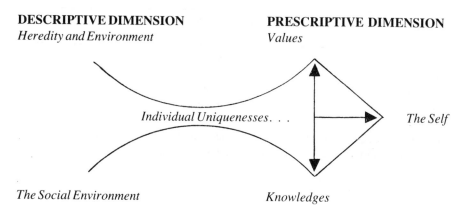

DESCRIPTIVE DIMENSION
Heredity and Environment

PRESCRIPTIVE DIMENSION
Values

Individual Uniquenesses. . .   *The Self*

The Social Environment   *Knowledges*

THE HESTER MODEL FOR INVESTIGATING HUMANNESS
FIGURE 2

Several keys to the successful development of inquiry lessons relative to this curriculum model are the following:

1. The academic preparations of teachers, stressing content and methods;

2. The ability of the teacher to blend knowledges, values and/or moral reasoning, and inquiry skills into each lesson; and

3. The use of the appropriate language patterns/actions of the descriptive and prescriptive dimensions of knowledge and understanding.

Figure Three defines many of the language patterns/actions characteristic of the curriculum model presented in this chapter. Their appropriate use will aid the students in understanding the areas of the curriculum presented to them. The consistent use of these language patterns/actions will add clarity and precision to class discussions and greatly improve the inquiry process.

LANGUAGE ACTIONS CHARACTERISTIC OF THE DESCRIPTIVE AND PRESCRIPTIVE MODES OF THOUGHT

Descriptive Language	Prescriptive Language

TO:
    differentiate
    describe
    characterize
    define
These language actions are based on memory and seek to give an account of a body of facts
	TO:
	    prescribe
	    direct
	    govern
	These language actions seek to advise, manage, control, influence, or regulate a body of knowledge or set of actions.

TO:
    locate
    discover
These language actions are based on using a body of facts and are designed to find out or make known.
	TO:
	    correct
	    modify
	These language actions seek to set right, improve, change, or alter a body of knowledge or set of actions.

TO:
    explain
 	
This language action seeks to interpret or render intelligible a body of knowledge, a process, or an event.
	TO:
	    evaluate
	    choose
	These langauge actions seek to appraise the worth of an idea or a thing.

FIGURE 3

THE DESCRIPTIVE DIMENSION. . .

An integrated and comprehensive study of what makes one a human rather than some other kind of being brings together the biological and sociological contexts of human development. A primary assumption of this curriculum is that there is no cultural development which is independent from a person's biological being. Also, an individual disassociated from culture is both a physical and social abnormality. One cannot artificially separate the biological and sociological areas of human life. Coupled with a person's individual life experiences, they are inseparable with regard to the essential uniqueness of what a person is or can become.

It is as though one begins the study of humanness by looking through a kaleidoscope at the bits and pieces of colored glass falling into particular patterns to form images. One notices the biological and cultural adaptations, the physical developments. And, as the tube is turned, the tumbling elements of human evolution yield ever a closer look at human invention, imagination, and discovery—at configurations which one labels "magic," "myth," "experience," "science," or "the arts." As the kaleidoscope continues to turn, one sees the future become the past, and new images of humanity continue to appear.

An important ingredient for our evaluation is that the person turning the tube (the human element) is participating in creating his/her own future and futures for generations yet to be born. Thus, it appears that a person has some control over who s/he is and how s/he is to be studied. But, at the same time, the patterns which appear in the tube are not entirely of one's own making. One is both in control and not in control of one's life.

Now is the time we must face the age-old question of whether human history is accidental or purposeful. Through the study of the factual, the philosophical begins to loom toward us. But the attempt to answer this question should be postponed until the facts have been studied. Answering this question is the responsibility of the prescriptive dimension of the curriculum model.

For the descriptive dimension, the search for facts is the first priority. This area of the curriculum model will be called Conceptual Scheme One: Emerging Humanity (see Figure 4). Its main purpose is to give an account of the bio-social facts of human life in general and of each individual life in particular. The relationship between the biological and the sociological dimensions of humanness lies in the vast domain of human consciousness. By studying the interrelatedness of these processes, the student will be better prepared to answer the question, "What is human about humans?" Also, this study will provide a context in which each student can pursue other nagging questions about the self, work on developing a personal set of values, and appraise the methods traditionally used for the acquisition of reliable knowledge.

THE PRESCRIPTIVE DIMENSION. . .

As was mentioned earlier in this chapter, the prescriptive area of this curriculum model is primarily evaluational. Once the student has become acquainted with the various facts that have set in motion the emergence of human life, then a descriptive foundation will have been established so that each student will have the opportunity to re-assess the major components of his or her life and of human life in general. These components include the self and self-awareness, values and morality, and ways of knowing.

It is not enough to study the basic themes and theories that scholars have developed regarding the evaluational dimensions of humanness. The student must also **RETHINK** his or her own personal **CONCEPTUAL UNIVERSE** and adopt ideas, values, and ways of living which reflect an intelligent appraisal of these fundamental components of human life.

The prescriptive dimension of this curriculum provides both teacher and student an opportunity to re-evaluate these three key aspects of humanness. The application of one's energies to this study will provide a conceptual background for one's future studies and for a life immersed in continual self-appraisal.

The curriculum model presented here represents a delicate blending of both the factual and evaluational dimensions of human life. Together, the study of these two dimensions will provide a very powerful cohesive and integrating part of the student's total education. They will aid the student in developing, modifying, and improving his or her own way of living. In the curriculum model presented in this chapter (see Figure Two) these two areas are major conceptual schemes. These conceptual schemes can be further subdivided into teaching units for application to the regular classroom curriculum or as independent units of study. By combining the descriptive and prescriptive areas, this curriculum model can be divided into the conceptual schemes and units illustrated in Figure 4.

PROGRAM AREAS AND UNITS
The Four Conceptual Schemes
Derived From The Curriculum Model

I. Conceptual Scheme One: EMERGING HUMANITY
    Unit Areas:
    1. Heredity and Environment
    2. The Social Environment
    3. The Uniqueness of the Individual

II. Conceptual Scheme Two: THE SELF AND SELF-AWARENESS
    Unit Areas:
    1. The Concept of Self
    2. Social Interactions
    3. Responsibility, Free Will, and Meaning

III. Conceptual Scheme Three: VALUES AND MORAL THINKING
     Unit Areas:
     1. Values and Normative Behavior
     2. Morality
     3. Principles of Socio-Political Thought

IV. Conceptual Scheme Four: KNOWLEDGE AND UNDERSTANDING
    Unit Areas:
    1. Sources of Knowledge
    2. Developing a Criterion of Knowing
    3. Inquiry Skills Development

FIGURE 4

5 CONCEPTUAL SCHEME ONE: EMERGING HUMANITY

GOALS AND OBJECTIVES

SCHEMATIC GOAL:

Students will explore answers to the question, "What is human about humans?" by studying the biological and sociological contexts in which humanity has arisen.

This study begins with the examination of the bio-cultural facts that have made possible the development of humanity as it is known today. This examination has been divided into three teaching units, each of which develops a different area of the descriptive study of humanness. Each of these three units will specify the knowledges, concepts, affective objectives, and inquiry skills which will be emphasized during the study.

When the units of this curriculum model speak of "knowledges," they will be referring to "those things which are known to be true." This definition will cover both basic knowledge and those facts which can be inferred from basic knowledge.

On the other hand, when these units refer to "concepts," they will mean "an idea or notion of what a thing is in general." This means that each concept ought to be analyzed in detail by students for complete and clear understanding. In the analysis of concepts, questions of fact and value must be clearly distinguished from questions seeking meaning and usage. For example, consider the following three questions:

1. Is it inevitable that Communism will spread all over the world?
2. Is Communism a desirable system of government?
3. Is Communism compatible with Democracy?

The first of these questions is a question of fact. One cannot give a direct answer because it seeks a prediction; the only relevant evidence for one's answer consists of facts about Communism and about the world.

The second is a question of value. To answer it one must assign some kind of value to Communism. One is being asked if Communism is good, bad, wise or unwise, morally right or morally wrong, politically desirable or politically undesirable.

The third is a question of concept. Here one must have some idea of the natures of Communism and Democracy. This goes beyond the meaning of the two words, "Communism" and "Democracy," beyond the various types of each system that exist in the world today, and beyond the consideration of the values of each system. Here one must determine whether or not the political systems of Communism and Democracy are logically compatible. To do this one must possess knowledge of the general characteristics of both systems.

In studying concepts one is dealing with the meaning and usage of words. In teaching for concept-understanding, it is not enough that the teacher separate questions of concept from questions of fact and questions of value. The teacher must also discover the following:

— the meanings various people give to the concept,
— a commonality of opinion among members of the class, and
— the appropriate applications of the concept in the real world of people, places, and things.

It is only when these three tasks are completed that the logical implications of the concept can be determined.

SUGGESTED CURRICULUM OUTLINE. . .

Below is a suggested curriculum outline which will help students deal with the topics or ideas contained within the schematic unit: EMERGING HUMANITY. The objectives listed under each unit follow the procedure explained in Chapter One of this book under the heading: "An Understanding Continuum" (see Figure 1).

I.   UNIT ONE: Heredity and Environment
      UNIT OBJECTIVE:
            Students will identify the various components of heredity and environment which are the building blocks of human life.

TASK DESCRIPTIONS:
A.   KNOWLEDGES
     Students will...
     1.   Identify common theories of human origins.
     2.   Locate and illustrate facts about human hominid ancestors.
     3.   Tell how biological inheritance produces variations in human beings.
     4.   Tell why all earthly life forms exist in ecological interdependence.
     5.   Differentiate human physical characteristics from those of other primates.
B.   CONCEPTS
     Students will define the following terms:
     1.   Living thing
     2.   Homo Sapien
     3.   Ecology
     4.   Heredity
C.   VALUES
     Students will...
     1.   Demonstrate a willingness to examine several points of view on a given subject before forming an opinion.
     2.   Identify the weaknesses and strengths of their own beliefs as well as those of others.
     3.   Tell why the physical environment ought to be preserved.
     4.   Identify the value judgments in the ideas and theories of others.
     5.   Demonstrate a problem-solving, inquiring attitude.
D.   SKILLS
     Students will...
     1.   Distinguish theories which are supported by factual evidence from those which are not.
     2.   Formulate hypotheses based on relevant evidence.
     3.   Draw conclusions from comparisons of likenesses and differences.
     4.   Scientifically classify various plants and animals.
     5.   Formulate generalizations by logically connecting specific bits of factual and conceptual information.
     6.   Evaluate hypotheses by their internal consistency and by their factual support or lack thereof.

II.   UNIT TWO: The Social Environment
UNIT OBJECTIVE:
   Students will identify the human social environment, heredity, and the physical environment as sources of human life.
TASK DESCRIPTIONS:
A.   KNOWLEDGES
   Students will...
   1.   Identify the social groups from which they have learned specific patterns of behavior.
   2.   Name the universal characteristics of culture.
   3.   Compare the individual differences in their culture with those of at least two other cultures.
   4.   Tell why language is important in acquiring and spreading cultural behaviors.
   5.   Name the major institutions of their society.
   6.   Identify the functions of their society's major institutions.
   7.   Compile a list of their society's most urgent social and physical problems.
   8.   State ways in which modern technology has changed human life in the past fifty years.
B.   CONCEPTS
   Students will define the following terms:
   1.   Society
   2.   Culture
   3.   Social Group
   4.   Socialization
C.   VALUES
   Students will...
   1.   Identify the major persons, groups, processes, and events in their lives.
   2.   Demonstrate a willingness to share personal problems relevant to the accommodation of social behaviors.
   3.   Show an awareness of the value of relevant social institutions, groups, and persons.
   4.   Perform actions which reveal positive values regarding other races, sexes, and ethnic groups.
   5.   Identify the need for the development of a positive humanistic and environmental ethic.

D.   SKILLS
Students will...
1.   Predict the logical implications of stated theories and hypotheses.
2.   Forecast events given the application of particular ideas, theories, and hypotheses.
3.   Judge the adequacy with which conclusions are supported by data.
4.   Appraise sources of information as reliable or unreliable.
5.   Demonstrate a knowledge of using graphs, charts, and numerical information to support theories and conclusions.
6.   Compare different pieces of information for logical consistency.

III.   UNIT THREE: The Uniqueness of the Individual
UNIT OBJECTIVE:
Students will tell why biological and cultural inheritance result in individual differences and peculiarities.
TASK DESCRIPTIONS:
A.   KNOWLEDGES
Students will...
1.   Tell why humans differ physically.
2.   Identify the influences of diet and nutrition on growth and vitality.
3.   List five to ten human characteristics which are instrumental in promoting the development of culture.
4.   Locate facts about the physiological basis of individual uniqueness.
5.   Locate facts about the chemical basis of individual uniqueness.
6.   Illustrate the mechanics of inheritance.
7.   Locate facts about the cultural basis of individuality.
8.   Identify basic human biological and psychological needs.
B.   CONCEPTS
Students will define the following terms:
1.   Pigments
2.   Stereotyping
3.   Anthropology
4.   Race
5.   Psychology

C.   VALUES
Students will...
1.   Formulate an answer to the question, ''What is the nature of being human?''
2.   Demonstrate respect and value for individual behavioral and biological differences.
3.   Identify both physical and cultural determinants of behavior.
4.   Show concern for the welfare of others.
5.   Demonstrate commitment to social improvement.
6.   Formulate an answer to the problem of human free-will.

D.   SKILLS
Students will...
1.   Appraise the advantages and disadvantages of being human.
2.   Identify similarities and differences within and among various human groups.
3.   Develop hypotheses about the effects of culture on individual differences.
4.   Compare student hypotheses about the effects of culture on individual differences.
5.   Synthesize the student hypotheses about the effects of culture on individual differences by creating a new theory from these various sub-theories.
6.   Debate the issue of free will versus determinism with other members of the class.

How Free Is Man?

When answering the question, "What is human about humans?", the issue of free will versus determinism is bound to arise. Few words in the English language have been used in so many different ways and with so many varied meanings as the word "freedom." When students use this word or when they begin asking questions about the nature of freedom, teachers need to be sure what sense of the word "freedom" is being employed by them. Following are several fundamental usages of the word "freedom:"

(1)   **Physical Freedom**—This usage means the freedom to move or travel from one place to another. Students in school may think that they have very limited freedom of movement. This sense of "freedom" can be explored and reasons given for limiting such freedom or giving more of it to some students.

(2)   **Psychological Freedom**—Freedom is often used to express the idea of being able to freely state thoughts or to react spontaneously to remarks made by other people. The idea of thought control may arise in the classroom and should be explored by the teacher. Examples such as propaganda and TV commercials will be excellent to explore.

(3)   **Civil Freedom**—The first ten amendments to the United States Constitution (the Bill of Rights) makes provision for certain civil freedoms. These freedoms give one the right to act within the framework of the law. In connection with the idea of free will, these freedoms can also be effectively discussed with the class.

The teacher should notice that the concept of freedom in relationship to the first three types of freedom carries with it the idea of responsibility. Such terms as "should," "ought," "praise," and "blame" are often used in connection with these freedoms.

(4)   **Freedom of Choice**—The philosopher is basically interested in the freedom of choice, that is, the capacity to choose freely between two options. It is this capacity which is at issue in the problem of free will and determinism.

Freedom of choice is the concern of this problem. This does not mean that philosophy is not concerned with freedom of press, freedom of religion, freedom of speech, or moral freedom. Rather, the philosopher feels that before these other freedoms can be addressed in a rational manner, the issue of freedom of choice must be clearly assessed. The more basic question of whether man is free in the sense that he or she has some power to choose between alternatives and to initiate action needs to be faced squarely by teachers and students.

The alternative to freedom of choice is determinism. This issue has far-reaching consequences. If a person's every thought and action are rigidly determined by forces beyond his or her control, then no one can act differently from the way he or she does. No one can really guide the course of their own lives. If a person could not act differently, should that person be held responsible for his or her conduct?

The implications of the solutions to this question touch on every aspect of human living. The idea of human nature, the power of self-discipline, the status of moral responsibility, personal relationships, and creativity are intimately connected to this issue. The question is, "Is everything determined?" That is, "Does everything have a natural cause?" "Does the universe and all of its parts participate in an orderly causal sequence?" The paradox appears when in our personal relationships we take freedom for granted, whereas in the sciences, we assume that necessity and determinism are the rule.

There are three basic positions that one might take with regard to free will and determinism. As a teacher, you will want to share these equally with your class. Share each position thoroughly pointing out the strengths and implications for each one. You may not necessarily believe that one or another of these positions is true, but dutifully go through each one of them so that the student will be able to give each position his or her serious consideration.

Position One—The Denial of Freedom:
For the most part, the natural sciences accept the postulate of hard or extreme determinism. This is the position that everything has a cause, including man. That is, everything in the universe is governed by natural and causal laws. The laws of causality which govern nature also govern the thought processes and behavior of human beings. Thus, whatever happens at a particular moment in time is the outcome of something that happened at a previous moment in time.

Thus, the entirety of our conscious lives, including our choices and decisions, are merely the expression of unconscious urges and desires. And, if a person's desires and actions are so rigidly determined, then that person cannot be held responsible for them. The person is merely the tool of unknown social and natural forces which are operative in the universe at any given moment of human existence.

Implications:
(1) We may think that we are free because we are conscious of most of our actions. Also, because we are ignorant of the real causes of these behaviors we assume that we caused them.

(2) All events can be explained as the result of direct cause and effect. Thus, moral terms like "ought" and "should" and moral praise and blame have no real place in the human world.

(3) Fatalism is often the result of the position of extreme determinism. It is the view that some, and perhaps all, events are irrevocably fixed. This means that human effort cannot alter them. Whatever happens is already predetermined at the beginning of time, independent of man's choices and actions. Thus, the future—rather than being open—is always beyond man's control.

Position Two—Indeterminism:
As a teacher, you may be completely turned off by the position outlined above as "hard determinism." This is understandable because it is your responsibility to open future possibilities for your students; to show them alternatives and help them make creative and enduring choices. Likewise, your students may also wish to reject this position. When this occurs, force yourself to remain objective. Examine the position of hard determinism thoroughly and the many reasons why it is held by the scientific community.

A position somewhat more compatible with freedom and decision-making responsibilities is that of soft determinism or indeterminism. This position justifies itself by pointing out that nothing can be more certain than what is given in a person's immediate experience. Because a person's experience of freedom is a part of his or her immediate experience, it has intuitive certainty and must be accepted.

The philosopher William James, in his essay, "The Dilemma of Determinism," shows how judgments of regret and tragedies such as murders present a real dilemma for the hard determinist. If the murder has been fully determined by the rest of the universe, a judgment of regret seems inappropriate, inconsistent, or foolish. That is, why would nature predetermine the murder of a person and predetermine a response of regret toward this event? What consistent cause could it possibly have?

Implications:

(1)   The position of indeterminism leaves open feelings such as regret, praise, and blame. These feelings imply that someone could have completed a certain action or prevented another action; that the future is open and that we create the future by our choice-making capacities.

(2)   This position also consistently allows moral responsibility. This does not mean that we are directly responsible for everything that occurs in the universe, but that we are responsible for those behaviors which originate within us and by us. Here "ought" implies "can."

(3)   Finally, the position of indeterminism ignores and denies the possibility of natural and social causes which fully or in part determine human actions.

Position Three—Moderate Determinism:

In facing the problem of human choice capacity (the issue of free will versus determinism), your students may square off on one extreme side or the other. Some of them will express a passion for freedom of choice and declare that the doctrine of determinism is completely false. Others will be impressed by the evidence of determinism, the scientific method and the like, and claim that freedom in the sense of personal choice is an illusion. They should be encouraged to investigate these two positions and debate them thoroughly.

There is a third possible point of view with regard to this issue, the claim that the real truth of the matter lies somewhere between these two extreme positions. The supporters of this third position say that the issue is not an "either-or" conflict. One does not have to accept freedom alone or fatalism alone. Rather, it is a "both-and" issue. This is the position of moderate determinism.

The position of moderate determinism acknowledges that determinism in some form is a vital scientific postulate. But, it points out that there are many different kinds of causal relationships. There are causal relationships which lie in the physical realm such as gravitational, electromagnetic, chemical, and mechanical. There are also organic causal processes which are directed toward the maintenance of the organism as a whole. In the realm of human behavior, there are geographical, biological, psychological, social, and cultural determinants. One event can be explained differently by a combination of these causes.

Yet, even in the physical sciences, the Heisenberg Principle—the principle of uncertainty—has returned some freedom to the universe and to human affairs. Henry Margenau, an outstanding physicist, tells us that the change from Newtonian physics to recent quantum theory has cast new light on the problem of freedom.

The position of moderate determinism links determinism and freedom and stresses the causal effectiveness of man's participation in world events. On this view, man is not only a creature of his environment; he is also a critic and a creator of his environment. This position holds that man as a self-conscious being has the ability for personal initiative and response. He is a center of creativity and within limits is able to reshape himself or herself, influence the behavior of his or her associates, and redirect the processes of the outer world.

Questions:

1. What qualities do you consider necessary if persons and societies are to achieve optimum conditions necessary for self expression?
2. Which position outlined above do behavioral objectives imply?
3. Examine the death of Socrates. Was he free or causally determined or both when he held to an ideal even though it meant death?
4. Distinguish between a dog, a stone, and a human being insofar as self-determinism and freedom are concerned.
5. Discuss: Since man does not ultimately shape his or her own character, it follows that he or she is not morally responsible.

INTRODUCTION TO THE PHILOSOPHICAL PROBLEM SHEET APPROACH TO PRE-COLLEGE PHILOSOPHY

The Philosophical Problem Sheets (PPS) are designed to stimulate and sustain student interest in the art of philosophical thinking. Philosophical thinking both promotes attitudes of objectivity and follows the canons of inductive and deductive reasoning. It addresses many of the fundamental issues that plague our society. The following simple procedures should be employed when using the PPS approach.

1. The PPS approach is designed to be used in conjunction with regular classroom course content. That is, the Hester Model for Studying Humanness and the PPS activities should be plugged into "natural" education sockets. The PPS activities serve as built-in motivators for classroom discussions and extra-class investigations.

2. Before using the PPS activities the teacher should thoroughly acquaint her/himself with the chapter (units and philosophical problems) which accompany them.
    The student's understanding of these philosophical problems is important. The student should understand how each of these problems fits into his or her life situation; that answers to them are at once personal and societal, oftentimes with strong ethical overtones. Also, the student should be encouraged to employ both logical and creative decision-making techniques when solving these problems. The use of investigative techniques, brainstorming, searching for alternative solutions, and rational debate are excellent skills which the gifted student needs to develop.

3. The teacher should encourage all students to participate in the investigations, discussions, scenario writing, and debates which lead to the completion of each of the Philosophical Problem Sheets.

4.   Fourth, before concluding the study at hand, encourage each student
      to investigate the problem in more depth. Prepare an adequate bibliog-
      raphy of all the materials you can discover on the problem. Have your
      students prepare a written investigation of the problem, their answer,
      and facts/reasons to support it.

It is important that the teacher make each student comfortable during the
investigation and discussion of each Philosophical Problem Sheet. The
teacher's objectivity and neutrality are imperative. The teacher should insist
that each student analyze and evaluate the possible solutions to the problems
posed by the Philosophical Problem Sheets before stating his/her own position. Learning the other positions, concepts, and their implications, is far
more important to the philosophical process than trying to decide which
position is "right." Being able to evaluate ideas, concepts, and values is
the first step in learning how to make rational choices and accept responsibility for one's decisions. The teacher's fundamental task is to help the
student learn to evaluate his or her own ideas. The teacher's role is to provide
support and encouragement to students as they begin to move from their
childhood world of absolutes to the more nebulous world of adulthood.
Learning to pursue alternative solutions to a problem, discussing biases and
"old ways" of thinking in a group setting, and articulating one's own
position help establish intellectual independence and life-long learning.

NOTE: This methodology will be used in the *Philosophy For Young Think-
      ers* activity books for each grade level.

PHILOSOPHICAL PROBLEM SHEET #1

Brain Drain

PROBLEM:

You are a member of a highly trained medical research team. For years you have obtained permission from dying persons to perform experiments to keep them alive. However, in nearly all cases, your best efforts have delayed death for only a few short months.

Today, your group was introduced to Steve. His body is diseased and unable to defend itself from various diseases or viruses. The organs have begun to malfunction. His body is incapable of keeping him alive. Soon Steve will die.

Pleas from Steve's parents have attracted your attention. They insist that a possible alternative to death would be a brain transplant. Planting his brain into the body of a person whose own brain is diseased would keep Steve alive. This operation has never before been tried, but the technology is available to your medical team. Steve has agreed to the surgery if a donor body can be located.

As you consider the surgery, several concerned individuals expressed some possible outcomes if the operation is performed.

Dr. Stevens stated Steve would be the same Steve that people now know since the brain determines who we are. Only the body would be different from the old Steve. His thoughts and emotions would be the same as before. Steve's friends would need to adjust to seeing a new Steve. Counselors would work with Steve to help him begin to understand his new body.

Dr. Watts argued that Steve's brain in a new body might not be the same as Steve as he was known. Instead, this combination could result in a person who had some of Steve's characteristics and other characteristics which Steve did not possess previously. Perhaps a personality develops in a combination of the brain and body. Who knows how much of Steve would be left?

Dr. Seymour maintained that the reaction might completely alter Steve's personality. In this case, a new person would be created. Dr. Seymour then asked the question as to whether the surgical team was willing to partake in a situation that might actually create new life?

ACTIVITY:
You and your surgical team have been debating the above issues and many others for several days. Finally, a call comes from the hospital. A victim of a car crash has been declared "brain dead." His parents have agreed to allow the team to try a brain transplant. You have the chance to give Steve the possibility of a new life.

After much debate, the team decides to operate. However, before the operation begins, your team must clarify what they think will happen to Steve after the operation. The team has agreed to consider the possibilities enunciated by Doctors Stevens, Watts, and Seymour.

Make a choice from their positions. Give two reasons to substantiate your decision. After you have completed your work, meet as a group. Try to come up with a group decision. Be prepared to debate this issue!

QUESTIONS:
1. What is Steve's present condition?
2. What makes up a person's personality?
3. How would you describe the connection between a person's brain and a person's personality?
4. How was your personality formed?
5. How would you justify an operation like Steve's on ethical grounds?
6. Assume that the transplant is successful. What name should go over the grave of Steve's body?
7. Would you say the research team was attempting to play God? Defend your answer.
8. How might the decision to operate be affected if the donor body was female?

EXTENSION:
The previous scenario reflected the issue of the "mind/body" problem. Are the mind and body one distinct entity or are they separate? This has many implications, both philosophical and theological. Plato assumed that the mind and body were separate. Indeed, there was for him the body and the soul. Upon death, the soul would leave the body. Christians talk about a bodily resurrection. In this sense, the body and personality (soul) of the person will be resurrected together.

The issue goes far beyond simply a theological one. We often speak of a person's soul leaving the body or separating itself from the body during peak experiences. Indeed, music is said to move the soul, although it can be argued that some modern music moves only the body.

A good exercise would be to consider if there is a difference between mind/body and soul/body. Obviously, I have interchanged the two. Would the brain be part of the body? Does the mind then exist separate from the brain? Where would the mind be located? What would be its function?

Another good exercise would be to have a group come into your school and discuss some experiences they may have experienced "outside" the body. In addition, one should try to find someone who might give a skeptical retort to such descriptions.

This topic is very exciting and philosophically challenging. There are many resources available which would allow students to engage this issue in greater depth.

PHILOSOPHICAL PROBLEM SHEET #2

Cloning Around

PROBLEM:

The Commissioner of Baseball has called together a Special Commission to decide what may well be the future of baseball. The Commission must consider the case of a professional team, the Dallas Rangers, or as they are now called, the Dallas "Clones." You are a member of this special commission. The details of the case are provided below.

CASE #2184: During the past two decades, the technique of cloning has been developing at an incredible rate. However, the technique remained very expensive. It was very costly to clone new individuals, especially larger individuals from the animal kingdom. Large apes, gorillas, and humans were the most expensive to clone.

Finally, in 2014, the U.S. Government decided that further clone research was too costly. No new money was to go into clone research or production. Since then, clone technology has been used rarely in large animal reproduction.

For 21 years, Max Johnson had been trying to develop a World Championship baseball team. In the year 2015, Mr. Johnson, owner of the Dallas Rangers, decided to use the cloning technique to produce his future team. Now it is known that he planned to have his champion team by playing clones.

Since Max Johnson was and still is one of the world's richest men, money was no problem. In 2020, he received permission from several All-Star baseball players to create clones. Each of the All-Stars was paid five million dollars and each agreed never to talk about the clone operation. All the players kept their word.

Thus, in the 2041 Spring Training Camp, Max revealed his new "cloned" team. The clones resembled the individual All-Stars of twenty years before. These players played as well if not better than their originals. Better coaching and training practices made Max's Dallas Rangers an unbeatable team. It looked as though Mr. Johnson would, at last, get his World Championship.

The Rangers, now called the "Clones" by the press, are seldom defeated. At first, people packed the stadiums to see these great players, but because their skills are so great, the impossible has become common, and gradually, attendance at games has dropped. The excitement has gone out of the contest and the pennant race, because people already know who is going to win. So far Max Johnson has paid little attention to the criticisms of his team. He wants a World Championship at any cost. Still the criticisms have continued. Clearly something must be done.

ACTIVITY:

It was in response to this situation that you have been called together by the Baseball Commissioner. A previous committee decided that there were only five alternatives from which the Commissioner could choose. The task of your group is to rank the alternatives in order from most to least desirable. As presented to you, the alternatives are:

a.   Let the "Clones" continue to exist as they are. Mr. Johnson made use of the resources which were available and built the greatest team ever. Any other owner could have done the same.

b.   The Dallas Rangers "Clones" should be removed completely from baseball. The game was designed to be played with each team having a reasonable chance to win. Taking away the chance to win is ruining the game. The game should not suffer for the benefit of one team.

c.   A rule will be established saying clones would not be allowed to play baseball; the game was designed for individuals to come together as a team and not to be born a team.

d.   After Mr. Johnson wins his World Championship, the players would be dispersed to other teams throughout the league. This way, the "Clones" could continue playing baseball but not all on one team; the league would be better balanced.

e.   The clones would be allowed to stay on the Dallas team. However, only three clones would be allowed on the field at the same time. This would restore a better chance for victory over the "Clones" by opposing teams.

After discussing the situation and policies with your group members, you are to:

1. Rank order the five policies by placing a ''1'' to the left of the policy
    you most want the Commissioner to follow, a ''2'' by the next wanted
    policy, on to a ''5'' by the policy you want to be followed least.
2. Next, you are to reach a consensus with the entire class as to the rank
    ordering of these five policies. Follow the same procedures as listed
    above for your individual rankings.

QUESTIONS:

1. What is a ''clone?''
2. Is cloning a form of reproduction?
3. In the story, why did Max Johnson develop a ''clone'' team?
4. How is ''cloning'' related to the study of heredity?
5. What is the relationship between a ''clone'' and his/her parents?
6. Is a ''cloned'' human, human?
7. Would you like being a ''clone?'', A parent of a ''clone?''
8. If the government decided to outlaw ''clone'' research, would you
    support this?
9. Would you consider a ''clone'' to be a mutant?
10. What are the possible consequences of allowing ''clone'' research to
    continue?

EXTENSION:

The issue of cloning has become an ethical issue which is getting attention
from both scientists and lay persons. Cloning involves making an exact copy
of a particular being whether this be mice, or theoretically, humans. In
breeding, male sperm unites with an egg to form another separate and distinct
entity. With cloning, the complete chromosome make-up of either the male
or female is combined with an egg which has its nucleus removed, thereby
providing the egg none of the genetic material. The result is a copy which
has the complete genetic code of only one parent.

  Several issues should be considered:
1. It is necessary to redefine what is meant by human being and being
    human. Obviously, this cloned life does not share the method whereby
    humans have previously been conceived.
2. What ethical theories should be applied or developed to monitor clone
    research? Does our society wish to have the technology to clone hu-
    mans?

3. Is it possible that cloning could become a very valuable tool to use? Imagine the possibility of cloning a dog from a particular dog which was capable of incredible feats of sniffing for drugs. Would this be of great benefit to society?

4. Would the cloning of individuals be allowed in certain situations, i.e., a great and brilliant scientist who has exhibited the highest I.Q. ever recorded? Would it make any difference if this person had developed inventions and materials which made life better for millions and millions of people?

Many science classes are beginning to talk about the possibility of using cloning techniques. Perhaps a debate between someone who is pro-cloning and someone who is against cloning research could be arranged. Another interesting topic would be to find studies which are about cloned mice. How were the mice different from mice conceived in "normal" ways? Students could be encouraged to look at this issue based on their own interests and to apply their findings to the issue of cloning human beings. Perhaps a forum and panel discussion could be arranged to share the findings.

Animal Rights

PROBLEM:

The issue of animal rights is attracting attention throughout the world. The issue is whether animals have rights or are to be treated in any manner which is judged "appropriate."

Clearly, individuals are not allowed to be cruel to their pets. Individuals can and have been prosecuted for cruelty to pets. Others have been prosecuted for the abuse of farm animals, i.e., allowing animals to starve to death for no apparent reason other than neglect. For most individuals, these examples of cruelty to animals are clearly unacceptable.

The issue becomes more complex when animals are part of the food chain. Farmer Jones raises pigs for human consumption. These animals are used to make chops, bacon, and sausage which is sold in the grocery stores. Farmer Jones's methods of raising hogs for market are based on the finest scientific studies. The pigs' feet never touch the ground outside their "pig parlor." They spend their lives on concrete floors. Each pig is in a pen which will not allow it to turn around. The pigs simply stand and eat or kneel and sleep. This allows them to be prepared for market at a faster rate. The pigs are fed a special formula and are given shots to prevent disease. Indeed the pigs are kept in a very clean environment in order to reduce the spread of disease. When a sow is ready to have her young, she is moved to a larger area which will facilitate the birthing process. When the piglets are old enough, they are taken away from their mother, sold or placed in pens with other piglets. Here they are fed special food to prepare them to move into the adult "pig parlor." This scientific process has allowed American agriculture to be the envy of the entire world.

Some individuals have argued that pigs should not be treated in such a manner. They should be allowed to walk on the earth and do "pig things" until they are taken to slaughter. Still others have argued that the pigs should not be taken to slaughter but allowed to live out a normal life on the farm.

Another issue concerns animals which are used in experiments within labs. The argument could be made that experimentation on animals has allowed for the development of products which are safe for human consumption and use. In this sense, it is obviously better to test products on animals than humans. One such test is the Draize Eye Test, which is designed to test the toxicity of various compounds. Below is a description of a Draize Eye Test as described by Dr. Tom Regan, President of the Culture and Animals Foundation.

> Typically, six to nine albino rabbits are placed in stocks to prevent them from clawing at their eyes to dislodge the substances. Only their necks and heads protrude. The lower lid of each animal's eye is pulled away from the eyeball to form a small cup. Into that cup, the technician drops some milligrams of a substance to be tested. The eye is then held closed for several seconds. With a particularly caustic substance, the rabbits scream in pain.
>
> The other eye is left untreated to serve as a "control." The rabbit's eye is then observed at specific intervals to see how severe the irritation is. Is the lid swollen? The iris inflamed? The cornea ulcerated? Are the rabbits blind in that eye? The results are noted on charts in case someone files a lawsuit against the manufacturer. The rabbits are then destroyed.

This test is performed for everything from furniture polish to make-up. To present an example of the amount of testing which is done daily, it is estimated that 26 animals die every minute in the U.S. alone, to test new shampoos, hair sprays, laxatives and oven cleaners. Would it be possible for companies to share their data? Are all these tests necessary? Is the development of new cosmetics worth the death of an animal?

Finally there is the issue of trapping animals for use as furs. Perhaps you have seen the poster of a young fox staring at a camera with the caption reading, "Are you wearing my mother?" Obviously such an advertisement can be both powerful and offensive depending on one's point of view. However, several things are clear. Animals which are trapped are oftentimes caught in leg traps for hours or days. These traps cause extreme pain. Some animals have been known to knaw their lower legs off in order to escape from the trap. Some trappers now use traps which attempt to catch and break instantly the animal's neck thereby causing little pain.

This is not an easy issue. Many a dog and cat has been rescued from those "cruel" leg-hold traps. Perhaps the shoes you wear come from animal skins. Perhaps the food you ate for breakfast or will eat for dinner is from an animal or an animal by-product, i.e., cheese or milk. Does this mean that animals should not be killed? Should certain conditions be met in order to insure that animals which are used for food are killed in a humane way? Should animals suffer tests in labs which are obviously duplicated in other labs? What should we, as society, do concerning our treatment of animals?

QUESTIONS:

1. What are some of the ways animals are used in our society?
2. What is the Draize Eye Test?
3. What happens to the results obtained from this test?
4. What might happen if animals were not used for testing of products?
5. Are there other ways to test products rather than experimentation on animals? (This question might need some research work.)
6. Should animals have any rights? If so, what might be some examples?
7. What might be a "Bill of Animal Rights?"

EXTENSION:

This is a very complex and difficult issue. However there are sources which can provide information for students wishing to examine this issue in greater depth. One group to contact is:

People for the Ethical Treatment of Animals
PO Box 42516
Washington, D.C. 20015
(202) 726-0156

Other groups to contact are the companies which do testing on animals. Many products have the address or phone numbers to call to give comments about a product. The contacts could provide information on the company's policy towards animal experimentation.

One could also set up a debate on the issue of whether it is necessary to eat meat in order to obtain the protein for a healthy diet. Issues would center around the habits of a nation, convenience and usefulness of meat. This is a tough issue. However, it is an excellent issue to get individuals to think in terms of needs vs. comforts.

PHILOSOPHICAL PROBLEM SHEET #4
Human Needs

PROBLEM:
It is believed by many that aliens from other planets have been visiting our planet. Many believe that at first these aliens were interested only in the physical make-up of the earth. However, there has been some evidence in recent years that their interest may have shifted to humans. This includes the apparent interception of many human communications, transmissions such as radio and television. Rumors are circulating among many that first-hand encounters between aliens and humans are increasing at a rapid rate.

Several days ago, five teenage persons disappeared. Mysterious tracks near their car have yet to be explained. There was no evidence as to how or why they vanished. Reports of strange lights in the sky have linked their disappearance to flying saucers and alien creatures. However, among many serious people who report such sightings are those who believe the disappearance of the teens is a prank.

On the way home last evening, you also noticed some strange lights in the sky. Ignoring them, you continued your way homeward. Then, without warning, you found yourself in an entirely new environment. By some means, you were "beamed" aboard an alien ship. Equally surprising, you looked across the room to see the five teenagers sitting very comfortably along the observation deck rail.

Without speaking a word, an alien "speaks" to you. "We are seeking information about your planet's people. We know much about what and who your people are. Our data on the physical characteristics and behavior of humans are extensive. But we know little as to why you do what you do. Our data here are confusing."

ACTIVITY:
These five humans were asked to name the one thing that all humans need. This question resulted in five different answers. Rank order the following responses from the most important human need down to least important human need. Before beginning, you may need to define what is meant by "human need."

1.   Jackie argued that **SELF-ESTEEM** is the most important need. "Humans need respect for who they are. People want to be judged on the basis of who they are and/or what they provide for themselves, their family, or peers. This is not necessarily only physical goods, but can also include meeting the emotional needs of other individuals. When esteem is shared, people are better able to appreciate one another."

2.   Jamie stated that the most important need humans have is the **NEED FOR SAFETY**. "Humans need to feel safe. This includes not only safety within the family but also safety within the community, state, and nation. Being safe allows for other feelings to grow and mature."

3.   Danny stated, "A person's biggest need is **PHYSIOLOGICAL**. Humans need food and water in order to survive or develop any other consideration separate from their own struggle for existence."

4.   Kelly felt **LOVE** is the most important need. "Humans need to be loved and feel others care about them for who they are. By having love, they are not afraid to make mistakes for there will be someone who cares about them and overlooks their mistakes. Having love and sharing love creates the desire to do good toward others."

5.   Gale felt **SELF-ACTUALIZATION** is the most important human need. "Humans need to be able to make decisions for themselves and be comfortable with their decision even if it is not the most popular decision. They need to be able to solve problems for themselves and to be concerned with the needs of others as they search for self-centered answers. Being comfortable and satisfied with oneself—realizing the fullest of one's potential—is the most important human need."

After rank ordering your choices, share your ideas with others in your class. Be prepared to give reasons for your rankings.

QUESTIONS:
1.   What was the question asked of the five humans by the alien?

2. The five individuals named physiological needs, love, safety, self-esteem, and self-actualization as the most important human needs. Can you think of other human needs?
3. What would be the most important need(s) of a small child?
4. How do our needs/values change as we get older?
5. How might the fulfillment of one's needs better develop an individual mentally, physically, and socially?
6. Think of a country different from your own. How might the needs of persons there differ from your own needs?
7. Should there be a criteria for judging all personal/social values? If so, what are the components of this criteria? Give your reasons for it.

EXTENSION:
For those familiar with psychological development, it is clear to see that the previous activity was derived from Abraham Maslow's hierarchy of needs. For Maslow, each stage builds on the previous one with self actualization being the highest level of psychological attainment.

As students begin to seek information about the "self," it is crucial to have them read what some of the great thinkers have said about humans and being human. This exploration could start with Plato and include many of the thinkers who have been so critical in the formation of the Western Intellectual Tradition.

A special book to lead any investigation of the "self" and the mind is *Maps of the Mind*, by Charles Hampden-Turner. The book is readable and comes close to being a comprehensive, illustrated exploration of the major ideas of the human mind from ancient to modern.

A panel of psychologists, philosophers, and theologians could provide a most interesting panel discussion for students under the topic: "What is human about humans?"

PHILOSOPHICAL PROBLEM SHEET #5

I Sentence You To. . .

PROBLEM:
You are a member of a legislative subcommittee. Presently your committee is hearing proposals concerning the re-instatement of a death penalty for first degree murder in your state. This proposal does not make the death penalty mandatory. It would allow a prosecutor to seek the death penalty and a judge to order its execution.

Ashley Jones is representing "Citizens For Just Punishment." This organization is in favor or the death penalty. Ms. Jones presented the following summation of her argument.

"In conclusion, the option for the use of the death penalty must be exercised. There are several reasons for this argument. First, society should be free—on a permanent basis—of individuals who commit horrible crimes. Society is not free if it must pay for the incarceration of these individuals. This money could easily be used by society for more pressing and worthwhile needs. Moreover, all too frequently, murderers escape or are paroled and kill again. Most murders are committed by repeat killers—people who have killed before. The most important right in our society is that of the decent tax-paying citizen to safety and security, and we can go some distance toward guaranteeing that by executing cold-blooded killers. Secondly, allowing the death penalty in certain situations will act as a deterrent. In other words, people will think twice about committing a murder if they know they will die if they are caught. Thirdly, keeping killers alive is detrimental to our entire penal system. They are a bad influence on other prisoners who might be rehabilitated and made into productive members of society. They occupy space in our already overcrowded prisons—space needed to lock up other offenders who rob and injure people. Fourth, the framers of our Constitution established a system which was meant to work with the death penalty as the ultimate law enforcer; we are able to have the society which they envisioned only if we use the death penalty rather than unlimited police power to make our system work. They used the death penalty for many more crimes than we do today."

Mr. Jay Pollard, representing "Citizens Against the Death Penalty," argued that the death penalty should not be re-introduced.

"Society has progressed to the point that the death penalty should never be considered. Even though someone might commit a horrible crime, the taking of this individual's life would be a greater crime. It would require society to lower itself to the level of the criminal. It would require society to implement violence to control violent people. If these individuals are convicted, we should continue seeking a sentence which will keep these people behind bars and not living freely as dangers to society. What society wants is safety from these types of criminals. Actual life confinement would meet these goals. In addition, there is no clear evidence that the death penalty in a state reduces the incidence of violent crime. Therefore, the death penalty does not seem to be a deterrent to crime. Finally, although society will need to pay for these individuals to remain behind bars, it would be a far greater social expense for society to implement the death penalty. Therefore, I urge you to reject this proposal."

ACTIVITY:
You have heard the arguments from the representatives of both views. You must reflect on how you feel about the death penalty and what you think should become the law of the state.

You are to vote for or against the death penalty. State two reasons which justify your position. Share your views with others in the class. Be prepared to debate this issue.

QUESTIONS:
1. What is the argument of "Citizens for Just Punishment" for the death penalty?
2. What is the argument of "Citizens for Just Punishment" against the death penalty?
3. Assuming the death penalty is allowed, under what conditions should it be sought?
4. Is implementing a death sentence a violent act?
5. Debate the issue of whether the death penalty is cruel and unusual punishment. (Note: you must consider both "cruel" and "unusual" punishment together.)
6. How might society benefit by executing criminals who commit violent acts?
7. How might society suffer by executing criminals?

EXTENSION:

The death penalty decision represents a difficult position for society. It can be argued that these individuals should be made to pay the ultimate for violent, planned crimes. On the other hand, having society sanctify the taking of a life presents another set of issues.

The issue of "cruel and unusual" punishment must be considered. For example, the death penalty may be cruel punishment but it may not be unusual. Indeed, the number of people being executed is rising in the United States. Implementing the death penalty is not unusual.

There are many areas which deserve additional consideration. One topic to investigate would be whether the violent crime in states which have the death penalty has increased or decreased since the implementation of the punishment. Secondly, it might be interesting to learn the expenses the state must incur as a person goes through the various stages of appeal. Is it cheaper to keep someone in prison for a lifetime or pay the expense of various appeals? Another consideration is whether the issue of expense should make any difference.

PHILOSOPHICAL PROBLEM SHEET #6

Choice and Responsibility

PROBLEM:
Mark Jones is on trial, accused of murder and arson. He had a criminal record at a very early age. The prosecution has presented witnesses who testified that they saw Mark committing the crime and running away.

The defense attorney asked a hospital to run tests to determine if Mark has an XYY chromosome make-up. This chromosome type has been observed in a high number of male criminals. Since Mark has other associative characteristics—tall for his age, skin problems, and a moderately low IQ (85)—it was suspected that he might have this chromosome pattern.

An XYY chromosome make-up, coupled with these other characteristics, apparently affects a person's impulse control. Such individuals are unable to consider carefully alternatives to actions in pressure situations. They act impulsively and are prone to violence. Thus, since many criminals are impulsive, these individuals are more inclined—perhaps because of their chromosome make-up—to commit violent crimes.

The defense argued that because Mark was born with the XYY chromosome pattern, as the hospital determined, he should not be held responsible for his actions. In addition, the defense argued that although Mark may have actually committed the arson, responsibility for actions is based upon the ability to make a choice. Mark, because of the XYY pattern, was limited in his ability to make a choice. His freedom to choose the "right" over the "wrong" was greatly impaired.

During the final arguments, the prosecution argued that a serious crime had been committed. Mark Jones had committed it. Further, society should not be held responsible for the genetic make-up of such an individual. The state must imprison people like Mark in order to assure the safety of all people. "A man whose genetic make-up does not allow him the freedom to choose to do right must not be allowed the freedom to do wrong," the prosecuting attorney said.

ACTIVITY:
You are a juror and have been ordered to the deliberation room. You must decide the guilt or innocence of Mark Jones. Faced with delivering a verdict,

you must examine all the alternatives presented at the trial. The foreman has asked for your vote. Is he guilty or innocent?

Give two reasons for your decision.

QUESTIONS:
1. Why is Mark on trial?
2. What does an XYY chromosome pattern imply?
3. When someone exercises free will, that person is making choices from possible alternatives. When someone is predetermined to do an action, one is not making a choice but acting out of necessity. How would you use the terms "free will" and "predetermined" in discussing Mark?
4. How do we, as a society, determine responsibility for an action?
5. Discuss whether the needs of a society or the needs of an individual should have priority.
6. Some scientists maintain that the matching of good genetic patterns among persons would result in fewer genetic-based problems. What would be some pros and cons of this position?

EXTENSION:
The above scenario reflects the free will/determinism debate. Just how free are humans to make choices which will affect them and others. Is the universe like a great machine which is simply ticking away and playing out its predetermined course? Or, do humans, through their decision-making and actions, determine the scope and sequence of human affairs? Perhaps there is a combination of the two.

Determinism may not be just an heredity issue. Consider the following example:

A child is born, the fifth illegitimate birth in seven years for the twenty-two year old mother. None of the fathers provides support for any of the children. The only money she receives is from the government, and it is not enough to provide "proper" food, clothing, and shelter. In addition to all the other difficulties, the mother of the child has less than normal intelligence. She is not sub-normal enough to receive additional services, although it is doubtful she could hold a job even if she could arrange for child care.

What kind of life can a child growing up in this home expect to have? Will the children be determined from birth to have a difficult time achieving in school and in society? What kind of lessons might they learn from the streets? How will you expect their lives to progress?

Predetermination may involve both heredity or the genetic code, and the position one is born in a society. In this matter, if a child grows up in a terrible home without love and care, what should society expect? In another avenue, does society have the obligation to remove children from a horrible home and place them in a home where they will have a better chance to become good citizens?

Take some time and reflect on the heredity/environment issue. What role does heredity play? What is the role of the environment in shaping character? Should someone with an XYY chromosome who grew up in a loving home be more responsible for his actions than someone who had an XYY chromosome and grew up in a terrible home?

PHILOSOPHICAL ESSAY

Moral Objectivity

When one begins the process of moral justification, the approach will be that of offering good reasons for taking the moral point of view. These reasons will be based on observing human beings in their personal, social, and political relationships. Even when we take such care by using reason and example, we cannot hope to have complete objectivity in adjusting and giving grounds for our moral views.

The pure subjectivist tells us that there is no way of rationally resolving fundamental moral disputes, because moral judgments and moral principles cannot correctly be said to be true or false independently of the attitudes of at least some people. At the heart of this position lies a theory of indeterminacy which postulates the arbitrariness of the emotions and the implication that there is no moral bridge to break the individual's isolation. In short, there cannot be any common moral questions and above all, no common moral answers. In other words, morality rests on the emotions of the individual who has been moved to behave in one way or another.

But there are some who feel that fundamental moral disputes can be rationally resolved. Because moral considerations are relative to human beings, the problem of moral justification is reduced to the removal of practical indecision or doubt; to the possession of an adequate motive for acting morally rather than selfishly.

It is the conviction of those who wish to remove the subjective element, and thus, arbitrariness, from morality that if a person is willing to reason morally, then the element of individual human choice need not reduce the decision to one which is subjective and irrational. But, one must remember that "being rational" involves a basic human commitment, the commitment to be consistent in thought and action so that if one finds that his or her moral code involves one in inconsistency, the code is so far irrational and must, itself, be modified.

Our situation is just this: Our everyday moral beliefs, rules, and judgments depend for their soundness on certain fundamental principles, but we seem to be completely at a loss to give reasons (objectively) for these fundamental moral principles. The question with which we must come face to face, especially as teachers who enter into moral debate with students on a regular basis, is, are there any guideposts, any moorings for morals. Is it the case that there are no definite answers available or achievable in our moral accounting procedures?

Our task in the classroom is not moral engineering. It is not our job to goad or persuade students to choose one point of view over another and to behave in one particular fashion rather than another. Moral engineering is one thing; the critical assessment of a moral principle, code, or set of rules is another.

Modern psychology has taught us that human beings are partly self-regarding and partly other-regarding in their behavior. There is an element of indeterminacy in all that we say and do. There can be no completely objective justification or morality because no reasons can be offered apart from a person's feelings and attitudes. In the long run, whether it would or would not be in a person's true interests to be moral depends on the sort of person he or she happens to be.

Observation tells us that the human animal is a many-colored, many-sided creature. On some occasions he or she acts on the basis of emotion, and, on others, by rational procedures. There are many times when a person responds to external pressures. A person feels obligated to home and family, to country and to self. On some occasions one acts because of these obligations, or sometimes, out of fear of reprisal. But, even in the face of the many and varied reasons given for a person's actions, once a person has made a commitment to think critically and rationally, then there is a possibility that his or her morals may have an objective foundation. This is why teachers desperately need not only to teach their students basic thinking skills and rational processes, but to secure their commitment (subjective though it is) to live lives characterized by rationality.

If we agree that a person must make some subjective commitments in order to retain some element of objectivity in his or her moral accounting, just what is the nature of these commitments? That is, if morality depends on what sort of a person one happens to be, then what sort of a person is it who is able to reason objectively concerning the basis of morality?

Commitment #1:

The first commitment one must make in order to become more objective in his or her moral accounting, is a fundamental commitment to consistency in thought and action. This requirement is the requirement of rationality. The requirement of consistency means that the criteria of morality cannot be internally contradictory nor, on the other hand, should one misrepresent the cumulative knowledge concerning men and societies.

Commitment #2:

The second commitment is to prudential reasoning; that is, reasoning that is characterized by calm, deliberate, informed, judgments concerning action. This means that a person will be willing to seek out the best means to his or her ends; it also means that one will strive to make his or her value judgments in a "cool hour," in light of a clear understanding of what the relevant facts of the situation are and a careful consideration of the probable consequences of acting on the various alternatives.

Logically, following prudential reasoning is not a sufficient condition for moral reasoning in that its intention is directed toward the self. But, it is a necessary condition for reasoning morally. Of course, our interest is not only moral reasoning, but what is required of any person who enters into the process of justifying the moral criteria that he or she advocates. The problem of moral justification is not a problem of morality itself; it does arise from within morality because morality cannot justify itself. Rather, the problem of moral justification stands outside of the moral enterprise as an activity of appraisal.

Commitment #3:

The final commitment of the person who wishes to retain an element of objectivity when engaged in the process of giving reasons for his or her moral commitments is a minimal concern and respect for other sentient beings, their needs, and aspirations. For human beings to justify their moral principles and enter into moral agreements with one another depends on the acceptance by them of certain views about people, the universe, and ways of knowing. This acceptance, this commonality, leads one implicitly to categorize moral language in a certain way. It leads to mutual understandings.

Our obligation frameworks will be criticized, justified, and corrected by reference to our shared moral understandings which begin with the sharing of deep attitudes and judgments toward and concerning animals and human beings. These shared understandings may be extensive or meager but they must exist. Justification cannot find a foothold without them.

Thus, a moral framework can be justified by reference to shared attitudes of respect and concern for human beings and other living creatures which infuse many of our concepts with moral significance. These concepts con- stitute a common ground and common bond which make the evaluation of a moral code possible.

This third commitment is a nonmoral commitment. Morality is itself anchored on it but will take this minimal concern for other beings one step further to that of regarding other sentient beings as equal centers of desires and goals, or to that of regarding others as deserving equal consideration. For many, the concept of "equality" must be applied universally for a commitment to be moral.

Conclusion:

This is the very point of this essay: there cannot be complete objectivity in moral justification; there will always be some reference to the attitudes and commitments of the persons involved. This does not mean that morals are in fact divorced from reason and thus, are arbitrary. Neither does this mean that there is a loss of moral objectivity. The burden of justification, or giving reasons, still lies on the shoulders of the person who makes these commitments. S/he still must show that following the prescriptions of morality is a rationally superior pattern of behavior by comparison with those of selfishness. That is, moral justification becomes that of showing that a selfish person has good reasons for being unselfish—if one can be by choice—for else it preaches only to the converted.

Finally, the fundamental principle of objectivity in morals is that of "reconsideration." Thus, it becomes the responsibility of the person who wishes to justify his or her own morals to consider the other relevant commitments which s/he, in fact, acknowledges; to reconsider, to compare, to adjust, and then to apply those principles in the everyday world.

CONCEPTUAL SCHEME TWO: THE SELF AND SELF-AWARENESS

GOALS AND OBJECTIVES

SCHEMATIC GOAL:

Students will compare various theories of personality formation in order to create a concept of the "self."

This unit begins with an examination of the concept of "self" and then proceeds to examine the social forces which enrich or enslave self-development. Also, this study will focus on the idea that when people are treated as free, responsible, self-directed, and unique individuals, then the arena of human involvement will take on an added quality and a more effective posture.

Judging by humankind's contemporary social interactions and by what little is known about the distant past, the human animal is and always has been a social being. The formation of social traits is rooted deeply in the human biological nature, a nature which lacks instinctive ways of facing modern social issues. This calls for a long process of learning from others. Although nearly all primates, and a few other animals, are social in their habits, human beings have developed their social abilities more than any other species.

Human beings have developed the capacity to subordinate and control biological urges for the welfare of the group. For humans, the group is the basis of contemporary society. Thus, an adequate understanding of the characteristics and functions of the group will greatly enhance the understanding of the "self."

Charles Horton Cooley was the first social psychologist to use the term "primary group" to describe such associations as family, neighborhood, and children's play groups. According to Cooley's observations, these groups are "the nursery of human nature." Accordingly, this is where the essential elements of group loyalty and concern for others are first learned.

The characteristics of the primary group are:

1. Face to face interaction,
2. Sentiments of loyalty,
3. Identification,
4. Emotional involvement,
5. Close cooperation, and
6. Concern for friendly relations as an end in themselves, and not as a means to an end.

The primary group gives the infant its first acquaintance with humanity. According to Cooley, **HUMAN NATURE** is not an isolated phenomenon, but a group-nature. One becomes human only in association with other people. In isolation, individuals begin to lose their social and/or cooperative tendencies.

The process of becoming human is referred to as the act of socialization. Socialization has three essential elements:

1. The learning of cultural symbols (language). Language is important for the conceptualization of reality, the understanding of complex ideas, and the conveying of views and values.

2. The development of physical and mental health through the relationship of human affection. Affection is the basis of cooperation with others, normal sexual development, and the parental transmission of love.

3. The development of human intelligence through human interaction. Human interaction is needed for social and emotional growth, learning cultural folkways, mores, customs, and participation in society.

To explain the dynamics of socialization (the way in which humans acquire their beliefs, attitudes, values, and customs), Cooley developed the concept of the "looking-glass self." Essentially, this is the process of forming one's own self-image in view of one's imagination of what others think. Cooley says that people actually learn to evaluate themselves through the eyes of others. This process begins with the very first days of life and continues through adulthood. The persons to whom one looks for the formation of one's own self-image are called the **SIGNIFICANT OTHERS**. These people are significant members of one's family, school and play groups, and/or they play an important role in one's occupation.

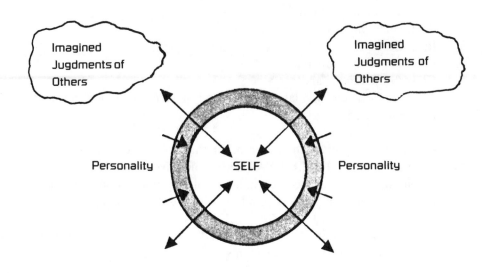

COOLEY'S THEORY OF THE LOOKING-GLASS SELF
FIGURE 5

An alternative to Cooley's theory is the hypothesis developed by George Herbert Mead. Mead says that personality is fashioned in early childhood as children learn to act out adult roles in play and games. This activity of learning traditional roles and accompanying attitudes seemed obvious to Mead.

Role-playing takes two definite steps:

STEP ONE: This step constitutes the internalization of adult roles. It may be simply playing the good guys versus the bad guys, or it could be emulating father, mother, doctor, nurse, or teacher. Mead maintains that there is a definite learning of traditional masculine and feminine roles during this first step.

STEP TWO: This step begins a more important aspect of the internalization of social norms. It is the development of the concept of the **GENERALIZED OTHER**. Children no longer play at pretend roles, THEY establish games with definite rules—the rules THEY have made up.

The indefinite THEY is what Mead means by the generalized other. This concept represents the rules and judgments of other people. Here are the beginnings of the understanding of others, the development of empathy. All the players in the game must learn the rules of other actors; here is where socialization begins.

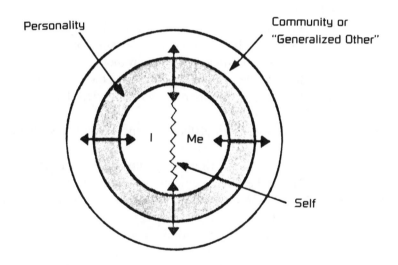

MEAD'S THEORY OF THE GENERALIZED OTHER
FIGURE 6

For Mead, the individual is not a complete pawn in the hands of other people. One uses the words "I" and "me" to mark two aspects of the self. The "I" is the subjective, imaginative, creative, and innovative side. The "me" is the objective side, the part that is largely formed through interaction with other people and groups of people. (See: Stewart, E. W. & Glynn, James A. *Introduction To Sociology*. York: McGraw Hill, Inc. 1974, pp. 84-85).

SUGGESTED CURRICULUM OUTLINE:
Below is a suggested curriculum outline which will help students explore
the topics and ideas contained within the schematic unit: The Self and
Self-Awareness. The objectives listed under each unit follow the procedure
explained in the Introduction of this book under the heading: "An Understanding Continuum" (see Figure 1).

I.   UNIT ONE: The Concept of "Self"
       UNIT OBJECTIVE:
              Students will distinguish the idea of "self" as a major concept
              whose purpose it is to guide and organize human behavior.
       TASK DESCRIPTIONS:
       A.   KNOWLEDGES
            Students will. . .
            1.   Identify self-development as a social process.
            2.   Name "significant others" in their lives.
            3.   Identify the role of "significant others" in their lives.
            4.   Define the various roles which society has established for
                 persons.
            5.   Give examples of the roles that society has established for
                 persons.
            6.   Identify the "primary" groups essential to their lives.
            7.   Name the three elements of socialization.
            8.   Give examples of the three elements of socialization.
       B.   CONCEPTS
            Students will define the following terms:
            1.   Significant others
            2.   Primary group
            3.   Socialization
       C.   VALUES
            Students will...
            1.   Demonstrate patience with their own capabilities.
            2.   Identify personal values in the activity of self-evaluation.
            3.   Demonstrate an appreciation for the role of others in their
                 self-development.
            4.   Display positive attitudes toward each other and their chang-
                 ing roles in society.
            5.   Demonstrate a commitment to social improvement.
            6.   Show a willingness to discuss status and role problems with
                 each other.

D. SKILLS
Students will. . .
1. Describe their individual concepts of "self."
2. Verbalize images of what they imagine others think of them.
3. Give examples of primary, secondary, and reference groups.
4. Compare the role of significant others in their lives.
5. Evaluate the changing significance of sex roles in their country.
6. Compare the changing sex roles of persons in at least three different societies.
7. Formulate an hypothesis about the role of others in personality formation.
8. Test their hypothesis about the role of others in personality formation.

II. UNIT TWO: Social Interaction
UNIT OBJECTIVE:
Students will conclude that personality cannot be understood apart from social interaction.
TASK DESCRIPTIONS:
A.   KNOWLEDGES
Students will. . .
1. Describe personal beliefs, values, and sources of knowledge.
2. Identify the significant persons, things, and events in their lives.
3. Generalize personal aims, ambitions, desires, and goals.
4. Differentiate between the kinds of people important to their growing personal environment.
5. Clearly state their attitudes toward significant others.
6. Identify the mores and customs of their primary group(s).
B. CONCEPTS
Students will define the following terms:
1. Looking-glass self
2. Generalized other
3. Cultural relativism
4. Norm
C. VALUES
Students will. . .
1. Demonstrate a willingness to evaluate their individual capacity for developing effective social relationships.

    2.   Participate in discussions of personal values.

    3.   Recognize the importance of attitudes and feelings about other persons.

    4.   Tell why friends are important as positive forces in the development of self-esteem.

D. SKILLS

Students will. . .

    1.   Differentiate certain people as important to their lives.

    2.   Classify personal wants and goals into a continuum of higher to lower priorities.

    3.   Demonstrate the ability to formulate and test hypotheses.

    4.   Illustrate on a flow chart the various inter-connecting areas of human interaction.

    5.   Summarize the views of the class on what is meant by "self-esteem" in order to create a composite definition.

    6.   Compare Cooley's and Mead's theories of the "self" showing points of similarity and difference.

    7.   Evaluate the consistency of the norms of one's primary group.

III. UNIT THREE: Responsibility, Free Will, and Meaning

UNIT OBJECTIVE:

Students will conclude that people are most effective when they are treated as free, responsible, self-directed, and reasonably unique individuals.

TASK DESCRIPTIONS:

A. KNOWLEDGES

Students will:

    1.   Create a set of goals for human development.

    2.   Suggest ways in which the goals can be implemented.

    3.   Identify three ways in which human behavior has been manipulated.

    4.   Identify the problem of dehumanization in modern mass society.

    5.   Make a list of criteria which they believe ought to guide human behavior.

    6.   Identify those activities that give meaning to life.

    7.   Identify those behaviors believed to be freely chosen.

    8.   List the sources of human determinism.

B. CONCEPTS
Students will define the following terms:
1. Human engineering
2. The meaning of life
3. Dehumanization
4. Social responsibility

C. VALUES
Students will:
1. State their beliefs about personal freedom or the lack of it.
2. Suggest a criteria for evaluating human behavior.
3. Identify those values which ought to be promoted among people.
4. Identify their feelings about different kinds of human engineering.
5. Demonstrate a willingness to discuss any feeling about one's own dehumanization.

D. SKILLS
Students will:
1. Evaluate theories of human development.
2. Write a set of human developmental goals.
3. Identify those specific areas of society which are dehumanizing.
4. Discuss the meaning and scope of social responsibility.
5. State the meaning of their lives in terms of present and future personal goals.
6. Evaluate the value of conformity and autonomy in a society.
7. Apply answers in this conceptual schemata to the problems of human identity and human meaning:
"Who am I?" and "Why am I?"

PHILOSOPHICAL PROBLEMS
"Who am I?"
"Why am I?"

I.   PROBLEM ONE: WHO AM I?

A person can have just as much trouble identifying himself or herself as identifying someone else. People are fundamentally unsure of their identity.

One reason for this state of affairs is that people get their self-image from concepts rather than from a specific group or a significant other. One reads that people are "fragmented," "specialized," or "encapsulated." One is told that humans today have no roots, no social stability. One does not know from where one came, why, or where one is going.

Without self-identity, a person is lonely and afraid most of the time. Life becomes meaningless. Seemingly, no one cares for us. After all, could anyone really care for a configuration of holes punched into a computer card?

What do life and death matter when the experiences of life and the finality of death are just a matter of statistics, of averages, and of highs and lows? Does the word "plastic" in some way summarize today's society?

These questions suggest an important philosophical problem, the problem of self-identity. When one asks, "Who am I?" or "Who are you?", the reference is always to a SELF. One says, "I think," "I should," or "I wish." In such statements a SELF concept is involved. What does one mean by the observation, "I am not myself today?" Can a person NOT be himself or herself? Or, is our language trying to tell us about certain changes in our self, personality, or mental posture?

If the concept of self is the center around which human life revolves, why are some people so insistent upon denying the reality of a "self"? Actually, a person cannot SEE a "self." One sees a body, but can only INFER the existence of a "self." Thus, how does one know, for sure, that the self exists?

These and similar questions can best be answered after examining the arguments which deny the existence of the self and those which affirm the self as a real and positive force in human life. Remember, if one chooses to deny the self, then those characteristics of human life normally accounted for by affirming the self must still be explained. If, on the other hand, the existence of the self is affirmed, then one must offer proof that the self is an actual entity.

SOME ANSWERS?

1.   CAN YOU DENY THE SELF?

Affirmation
The self is illusory. It is an outdated concept, too obscure to explain anything.

A.   THE BUDDHIST TRADITION
Traditional Buddhist philosophy asserts that nothing which exists is permanent. There is no permanent "soul" or "self." Rather, Buddhists believe in the AN-ATTA ("no-self"). "No-self" refers to the five processes or "skandhas" which come together to create being. They are:
1.   bodily sensation,
2.   feeling,
3.   perception,
4.   mental conception, and
5.   consciousness.
   If one were asked what is a wagon, the usual answer would be that a wagon is a combination of wheels, axles, wagon body, yoke, reins, etc. The Buddhist would give a similar reply if asked about the self:
      "The self is a combination of sensation, feeling, perception, conception, and consciousness."

B.   EMPIRICISM
David Hume (1711-1776) was unable to discover any "thing" that he was willing to label as "self." Introspection was able to reveal only fleeting sensations. Hume called these sensations "the empirical self."

Hume's Introspection

"For my part, when I enter most intimately into what I call MYSELF, I always stumble on some particular perception or other, of heat or cold, light or shade. . . I can never catch MYSELF at any time without a perception, and never can observe anything but the perception."

For Hume, the empirical self is not permanent. These sensations are always moving, always temporary. There is no NONMATERIAL substance or permanent quality called "the self."

C.   BEHAVIORISM
B. F. Skinner, the behavioral psychologist, says that a concept of self is not necessary in the analysis of human behavior. MENTAL EVENTS do not have the dimension of science. They cannot be verified by observation or by inference.

The concept of the free, inner self which is held responsible for the behavior of the external biological organism is a prescientific substitute for the kinds of causes found in scientific investigation.

Intentionality

One response is to deny that belief and fear are mental states. Rather, they are held to be dispositions to behave in certain ways. States of belief and fear "refer to" or "intend" something. My believing that you like me is not an occurrence at all. It is my being "set" to act in a friendly way toward you, to speak well of you, etc. Also, fear is not merely a feeling or occurrence; it is being "set" to run, to strike out, to be paralyzed, etc.

For Skinner, what one normally calls "self" is merely a symbol which represents a unified system of physical responses. Also, since motives, ideas, and feelings are NOT in principle observable, they can have no part in determining or explaining behavior.

There are many who agree with Skinner. They avoid words like "self," "mind," and "self-consciousness." Instead, they speak about stimuli, responses, intentionality, and behavioral biographies.

2.   CAN WE AFFIRM THE SELF?

The Concept of Self
Traditionally, that aspect of a person which ponders, decides, and initiates changes in that person's body. A body is not a human being until a "self" is added.

TASK: Compare the following positions with the statements above. Evaluate the strengths and weaknesses of all three. Then formulate your own hypothesis about the existence or nonexistence of the SELF. You should be able to support your hypothesis with good reasons and statements of fact.

A.   THAT WHICH PERSISTS. . .

According to this view, the self is "that which persists" throughout changing experiences. The "self" is an organism which can think, express emotions, and make decisions. It may or may not be a material substance. In either case it is the center of personal identity.

Personal identity includes that quality of uniqueness and duration through changes and time. Thus, the individual is able to say "I," "me," or "I remember." One may claim objectivity in science, but the person who makes this claim is a subjective entity. To deny our inner subjectivity would, therefore, result in a denial of any kind of objectivity.

B.   THAT WHICH TRANSCENDS. . .

Because people are able to integrate and synthesize their experiences (transcend them), there must be a "self" which is the center of this process and directs it to completion. People experience the world of other individuals, things, and events. They also experience themselves, their bodies, and their mental states. The continuity of the rational processes involved in reading or in writing a sentence implies a continuing self. This self is aware of its function. This inner self can also transcend time. Although bound to one's body in the present, my self—through memory—is able to consider the past, and—through imagination—meander around in futures yet to be realized.

C.   THAT WHICH IS PRIVATE. . .
This position gives three fundamental qualities to the definition of the "self." These qualities are PERMANENCE, TRANSCENDENCE, and PRIVACY. Thus, by its very nature, the self cannot be adequately described in objective terms. The self cannot be verified as scientific fact.

One can speak of his or her body, the environment, and home. One can give a body part to another person. But one cannot substitute the content of someone's personality and consciousness for one's own. One cannot feel someone else's pain. No one can directly experience another self. One can only INFER the existence of another self or IMPLY the existence of one's own self.

II.   PROBLEM TWO: WHY AM I?
A person often asks:
   "Why am I here?"
   "Why is there a universe?"
   "What is the purpose of life?"
   "What is my destiny?"
   "Is this life all there is?"

All of these questions focus on the purpose or meaning of human life. By "purpose of human life" one can mean "the conscious intention of people, groups or organizations." Or one may have a more cosmic meaning. One may be referring to the "meaning of the world" as if there might be a purpose for all of human life as viewed from a DIVINE perspective.

How people answer the above mentioned questions will often determine the direction and quality of their lives. Finding meaning in human life is considered to be a survival prerequisite for the human species. The concept of meaning will be individually defined and culturally differentiated.

SOME ANSWERS
Below are statements representing four different viewpoints regarding human purpose. After reading them, write a short paragraph in which you define

the purpose of your life. Do not limit yourself to anything written in this book or to any particular viewpoint mentioned here.

1. Are human beings subject to the laws of nature? Human nature is entirely a mechanical phenomenon subject to the laws of nature. There are no higher qualities in human life such as soul, self, or the image of God.

2. Are human beings subject to environmental influences? All behavior, human or otherwise, is controlled by the principle of operant conditioning. Human consciousness is merely a by-product of behavior and not something that makes human behavior different from other animal behavior. Ideas such as free will, the inner self, and autonomous being are inaccurate and useless concepts.

3. Are human beings rational creatures? The lower animals are like machines whose behavior is totally controlled by physical laws. However, human beings have both an animal and a rational nature. Their rational nature allows for judgment, choice, and free will.

4. Are human beings creatures of their own humanness? Human nature is distinct from and superior to animal nature. Every human being has the capacity to grow to an ideal form. This drive toward self-actualization can be changed or destroyed by a poor social environment. In addition, human beings have inner needs that other animals do not have. These include the need for love, self-esteem, recognition, integrity, self-respect, and self-understanding.

PHILOSOPHICAL PROBLEM SHEET #7
Doctor's Choice?

PROBLEM:

You are an accomplished physician practicing in the town of Meat Camp. When you were a teenager you decided to study to become a doctor. You worked hard in college and were accepted into Carolina Medical College. After receiving your initial medical degree you specialized in internal surgery.

When you took your oath as a doctor you pledged a responsibility to do all within your power to work towards the preservation of each patient's life and well-being. Throughout your medical career, you have maintained a high degree of medical ethics. You have often sacrificed time with your family to treat a seriously ill patient. You are truly a doctor devoted to your patients and their lives. You are often faced with decisions which must be made quickly and accurately. Tonight a situation has occurred with which you have not previously dealt.

Three members of a family have been critically injured in a car wreck. You recognize the lady as Ms. Zackery. She and her husband are the parents of five children and live in your neighborhood. Two of the children, Gabe and Sarah, were with their mother at the time of the wreck.

Quickly the hospital staff springs into action. After an initial assessment of the situation, you order blood. You estimate you will need a minimum of 15 pints of blood to assure the survival of the injured. You begin to prepare each patient to receive the blood. They must have blood before you can do any surgery. Suddenly a nurse appears. She informs you that due to a computer error, the hospital only has 10 pints of their blood type. It would take at least an hour to get more blood because all three have a rare blood type. Waiting could condemn all three to death.

You have never faced a situation like this before. The required needs (i.e., blood, personnel) have always been available in your previous medical experience. You have always had the freedom of giving each patient the best facilities and medical knowledge that were available. You have now lost that freedom. Your choices have been limited. You have a mother and two children in critical condition. It would be dangerous to split the blood three ways since all the injured could die. You are confident you could save at least two lives if you split the blood two ways. If the blood is split two ways, you must decide who will NOT receive blood.

ACTIVITY:
You have always maintained each individual has an equal right to life. The present situation has you puzzled and distressed. If you argue that each person has an equal right to life, then the blood should be split three ways with the possibility of death to all three. Obviously, your freedom of choice is limited by your present situation.

Time is short. You must decide. You turn to the nurse and say. . .

QUESTIONS:
1. What is the situation of the people injured in the wreck?
2. When a child dies before a parent, the parents grieve severely. Should this consideration affect what a doctor should do in a situation such as the above?
3. Define the term "freedom."
4. Define the term "responsibility."
5. What do the terms "responsibility" and "freedom" mean to you? Do these two concepts occur together or separately?
6. Define the concept "free will."
7. We often consider humans as beings with free wills. Humans also assume responsibility for their actions. In this case, is the doctor's free will restricted by what he views as his responsibility?
8. Suppose the doctor was able to phone the home of the accident victims and talk with the oldest child in the family. Should this child have input as to what the doctor does?

EXTENSION:
Assume the doctor made the decision to save only two lives. Could he be charged with neglect in the death of the other person?

Should someone at the hospital make every effort to reach the husband/ father and ask him for his input? Should this be strictly a medical decision?

What if the husband requested that the mother be saved, but the doctor determines that he could certainly save the two children with the available blood but has only a marginal chance of saving the mother? Therefore, he elects to save the two children. The husband then sues the doctor. Should the doctor be prosecuted for going against the wishes of the father?

Have the students think of a time when they had a decision to make when either alternative was not pleasant. How did they go about making this decision? How was making this decision like the decision a doctor might need to make?

Try to have someone from a hospital who has had to make some decisions regarding life and death—such as who qualifies for a transplant—come to the classroom. What criteria were used for the decision? What other factors—such as freedom and responsibility—come into play?

PHILOSOPHICAL PROBLEM SHEET #8

Bug-a-Boo

PROBLEM:

Recently there has been a discovery which could affect the health of large population groups. Individuals have been found who possess a rare viral infection which apparently has remained dormant for ages. When administered to rats, this viral infection quickly spread to other rats within the experimental laboratory. This rapid spreading was considered theoretically impossible with humans. However villages in remote parts of the world were reported annihilated by the virus. Apparently the emergence of this virus among a member of the tribe would quickly spread to other members. The mortality rate among those infected, which would be nearly all members exposed to the virus, was extremely high. Fifty percent of the individuals died within three years.

Simple examination procedures can be used to determine who is carrying the virus. However, just because one carries the infection in a dormant state doesn't mean one will actually develop an active case of the disease. Presently there is no known cure for this disease. For now the disease has not appeared in the heavily populated areas of the world. Perhaps the conditions which caused the infection to become active in very rural areas would not arise in modern nations. Indeed scientists are now presently studying how the disease went from a dormant state to an active one. So far, there are no leads. However, it is possible that if this disease was to spread into populated areas, millions of people would be at risk.

ACTIVITY:

You are a representative to the World Health Conference which will make recommendations to all world governments involving procedures to follow in handling this issue. The presented choices are as follows:

1. All the world's national governments would immediately test and isolate all individuals who have this dormant, yet possibly fatal, virus into areas which would not endanger the majority of populations. This would obviously break-up families but might save larger populations. The separation would occur until a vaccine is developed for the virus.

This would be an example of providing the greatest good for the greatest number of people.

2. Since the virus has not developed except in isolated rural environments, everything should be left alone to avoid panic among the masses. Hence, any research done involving this virus should be done in secret.

3. Researchers should continue to study the virus. Health officials should notify the public but stress there is no danger at this moment. In addition, wealthy nations would agree to pour money into research projects.

4. The public should be told. Ideally, people would volunteer for testing. If individuals were found to have the dormant virus, they would be urged to go into isolation until the vaccine is developed. This would help insure the safety of their families and others around them. However, under no situation would these individuals be ordered to report to isolation areas. In this manner, individual rights would not be violated.

After months of debate, these four positions were the ones the majority agreed their governments would entertain. As a group, the representatives have decided that they would recommend one and only one of the above positions.

As a member of the World Health Conference, you are to select the one policy you would want your government and any other government to adopt. State your reason and write two reasons which justify it.

Now, as a member of a group, you are to reach a group decision as to what policy your entire group believes must be followed by all world governments.

QUESTIONS:

1. In the scenario, what was discovered that could affect the future of the human race?

2. What are some examples of the disease's ability to spread?

3. What are some possible problems which could arise based on your preferred recommendation?

4. How could you justify providing the "greatest good for the greatest number?"

5. How do you determine the rights of individuals vs. the rights of the group?

6. Would it be moral for governments to hide health secrets from their people?

7. How would you react if your government had a policy to save certain people before saving others?

8. Would you consider all life and death decisions moral ones? If so, what criteria should determine the course of action?

EXTENSION:

This scenario obviously presents a difficult issue on which to reflect. Is it possible this scenario reflects in part the concern over AIDS? Obviously there are some differences. Scientists believe they know how AIDS is spread. Individuals who avoid certain behaviors reduce the possibility of obtaining AIDS. In addition, progress is being made in an effort to understand and perhaps develop a vaccine which would eliminate, or at least control, this horrible disease. However Health and Human Services Secretary Otis R. Bower stated in January, 1987, "If we can't make progress, we face the dreadful prospect of a worldwide death toll in the tens of millions a decade from now."

There are those who argue that those who test positive for the disease be isolated. This argument is based on the idea that those who have the disease can spread it to others. This clearly is so. However, many individuals who have the disease have been very careful to avoid knowingly spreading the disease. What do you think should be done? Carefully consider the need for individual rights, the knowledge and advances of science, and the needs of a society. What position should a government take?

Perhaps a good activity would be to organize a debate on the issue. Another idea would be to have a group of speakers come and discuss this issue with your class. This group could include citizens within the community, philosophers, theologians, and individuals from the medical profession.

PHILOSOPHICAL PROBLEM SHEET #9
A Soldier's Life

PROBLEM:

Joe was a soldier in the "B" Army. He has always wanted to be a soldier and hoped to make the Army his career. From the Army's viewpoint, Joe was a model soldier. One of the main reasons for their praise was that Joe always obeyed orders. A soldier is expected to obey all orders given by higher ranking officers. Officers are said to have a better picture of the overall objectives than enlisted troops. To assure success in an operation, the line of command runs from the top generals to the lowest ranking soldiers in the Army.

Joe was stationed in a foreign country fighting a war. Joe, like the natives of this country, had learned to speak some of their language. He would often give these people food in order to help them with their needs.

One day Joe was ordered to get up early. He and the platoon had a job to do. They were marched to a village six miles from the base. Joe had been there once before and knew several villagers. The lieutenant then gave the order:

"A couple of nights ago, a platoon was ambushed with heavy casualties. From this and other incidents, high command has determined this village has informants who are reporting our position to the enemy. From past experience, we know the informants could be boys, girls, men, women, young or old. Our orders are to destroy the village and all in it."

Joe had heard of this kind of operation before. He knew some of the people in the village. No harm had ever come to him during his visits. However, he had been given orders which were to be obeyed. He had always obeyed orders and trusted his superiors. He also knew a failure to obey orders would result in a court-martial and an end to his Army career. The order was given . . . move out.

ACTIVITY:

It was time for Joe to make his decision to obey or not to obey his orders to move out. Doing the best thing he knew to do, Joe stood up and . . .

QUESTIONS:

1. What is a good soldier expected to do?
2. What was Joe's order?
3. What was the reason given for the order?
4. What is the probable result of disobeying an officer's order?
5. Have you ever been asked to do something you felt was wrong?
6. Explain whether a soldier should have the right to disobey an order s/he feels is unjustified.
7. Suppose an order was issued from the top of command to execute some prisoners. The platoon carries out this order. Eventually this action is discovered. The press reports this and a nation is made aware of this action. Discuss who should be held responsible, the command or the soldier who carried out the order.

EXTENSION:

There is no doubt that individuals are told to do things on which they may disagree. This happens in business, industry and education! What should these individuals do? Consider the following example:

A diplomat from government A is ordered by an authority in the government to violate the laws of the country as established by the ruling body. The violation would involve the paying of money to a group which has killed many innocent people. However this group has information which may prove beneficial to government A. Clearly if the diplomat told government A's ruling body about this request, they would be very upset. However, this authority which wishes to have this information is one of the most important persons in government and works closely with the President. What should the diplomat do: Break a law of his/her country to get the information wanted by a high authority in the government, or refuse to break a law even though s/he has been told the government needs this information? Where should the loyalty lie?

Spend some time discussing this issue. It might be especially relevant to review some of the WATERGATE testimony and also examine some of the findings of the NURENBERG TRIALS at the conclusion of WWII.

PHILOSOPHICAL PROBLEM SHEET #10
To Draft Or Not To Draft?

PROBLEM:
Several students were sitting around a table debating the issue of a military draft. A proposed draft would involve taking nineteen-year-old men into the armed forces for a period of two years. Afterwards, these individuals would be free to return to civilian life or remain in the military. This draft would be on a lottery basis. All dates would be drawn out of the container. All individuals whose birthday was on the second date drawn would be drafted next, and so on. Obviously the military would not draft every nineteen-year-old male unless involved in war. Therefore the military would utilize only the draft numbers drawn, i.e., 1-75, in order to meet their needs.

Gene felt that the draft was unnecessary. "Why should I be drafted when our country is at peace? I have plans after high school. I want to go to college. This would interfere with my college plans. Actually if the draft was initiated and I was drafted, it would delay my college for two years. This is just too much time."

Dennis felt that the draft was fair. "What's the matter Gene? Don't you feel you owe some obligation to this country? After all, many people have fought and died for this country in order to allow us our freedoms. What is two years of your life in the service of your country? If the military needs soldiers, then a draft should be initiated. Besides, the training received would make it easier to call up troops in times of emergency. You already would have the training."

Sarah felt that a draft was appropriate, but why should this be a military draft? "I believe that there should be a draft but not just for the military service. There should be a draft which would place people in various services throughout the country. The people in this program would be like the VISTA volunteers (Volunteers in Service to America). For instance, some people would be drafted to work in areas where there is a great deal of illiteracy. These people would spend two years helping people learn to read. Other people could help in hospitals. Still others could help build housing for the needy. We would be paid a wage which would allow us the basic necessities but little more. This would allow us to give something back to our country.

In addition, this could be required for all mentally and physically fit nineteen-year-olds."

"Great idea Sarah," stated Howard. "However, for the sake of argument, lets assume that the military draft is the only available option. Shouldn't women be drafted into the military along with the men? Israel uses women in the military. It has been shown that women can take more 'G' forces in the cockpit of an airplane than a man. It seems to me that women could fight or do other military duties as well as a man. If women want to be treated equally by a society, then they should be willing to assume some of the risks and obligations that men may need to face. Saying that only men can be drafted seems like discrimination to me."

Other students began to join in the discussion. Many different points were exchanged by the students. Some felt that there should be no draft while others felt some sort of service to the country should be required for all individuals after completing high school, or for those who have dropped out of high school and are at least twenty years old.

ACTIVITY:
You have read the above problem. What is your opinion on this matter? Develop a position paper on this issue. Be sure to state the strengths of your position and the weaknesses of the other points of view. Students' papers should be made available for others to read. Afterwards, debate the issues within class. Note if your position or ideas have been changed by the arguments of others.

QUESTIONS:
1. What are the options regarding the draft?
2. Would it be fair to ask nineteen-year-olds to give up two years of their life for compulsory service? Why?
3. What might be some of the positive aspects of a draft for either the military or service areas? What might be some of the negative consequences?
4. What benefits might one reap from engaging in compulsory service?
5. Discuss whether the argument that women have equal rights to men and therefore should take equal risks, is sound. (One point might be that men do not take the same risks as women, i.e., birth!)
6. Would you consider it moral to require service based on a lottery where some may not be required for service?

EXTENSION:
This is always an exciting topic for high school students. Many students' fathers were drafted into the military and saw combat action. Others were drafted and did clerical duties. Many others joined VISTA or the Peace Corps. Still others chose to become conscientious objectors to military and do two to four years of alternative service to the country. Obviously these individuals had many different types of experiences. Parental reflections on their experiences may influence the student's view of this issue.

This would be a good time to involve some parents in the classroom. Find parents of students in the classroom who have military or VISTA type experience. Have them come into the class and share their experiences. Perhaps they could talk about whether they would wish their children to be drafted or engage in some service to their country.

Another task might to be to write U.S. Senators. Explain that you are doing a study on the possibility of compulsory service for individuals. Seek out their opinions. Try to develop questions which would draw out a Senator's philosophical stand. (Avoid yes or no questions.) Afterwards the results could be tallied and a report issued. This would give students the opportunity to come in contact with and reconsider the many philosophical positions that others have on this issue.

PHILOSOPHICAL PROBLEM SHEET #11

Ban The Book

PROBLEM:

Recently the (hypothetical) book, *Running in the Garden,* has come under attack by some people in Marketville. They have argued that the book has no place in the high school library. The book is a graphic representation of life for soldiers during the Vietnam War. The book tells the story of the soldiers in their own language which is oftentimes quite explicit. The book covers how the soldiers thought about God, religion, sex, politics, and social issues which were a part of their lives both in Vietnam and home. Four positions have been expressed by various members of the community.

Position I states that children, even high school-aged individuals, should not be exposed to such violence and language. This is a time when individuals begin to form ideas about the world around them. This book could cause a person to think that all the soldiers did was fight and think about sex. The book does not talk about why we went to Vietnam or the good intentions of our actions. Clearly, this book has no redeeming social values to teach. It could be argued that the constant use of God's name in vain would be reason enough to remove it from the library's shelf.

Position II states that the book is needed and should be kept on the library shelf for it gives an important perspective on the Vietnam War, which is rarely discussed—the ideas of the fighting man. Many books have been written about the political or military strategy. But few have centered around what it was like fighting in the jungle and in the villages. Some veterans have argued that this book has great value. Perhaps by reading this book, individuals will realize that war is not like the commercials on television, but rather is a violent action in which friends and people die. In this sense, one veteran, Joe Smith, has argued that the book should be required reading.

Position III states that no book should be removed from the library shelf unless it is pornographic in nature with no redeeming social values. This

means that a book which is very graphic in nature but attempts to portray
reality or an idea which should be considered by individuals ought to be
kept on the library shelf. Obviously, the idea of "redeeming social values"
has been greatly expanded from the position. This position holds that one
should examine all possibilities and ideas of individuals and cultures before
making decisions. The educated person is not someone who is immersed
only in one idea or one way of examining an issue. Therefore, "controversial" works are important to help individuals become more complete thinkers.

Position IV states that the book should not be removed from the library
shelf because it would be a violation of freedom of speech as guaranteed
by the First Amendment to the Constitution. There is no need to consider
any of the other positions because the Bill of Rights guarantees its place on
the library shelf.

ACTIVITY:
You have been placed on a committee which will decide whether the book
should be removed from the high school library. Clearly the town's feelings
on this issue are running quite high although there is a great divergence of
opinion over what to do. Your committee has agreed to use the four positions
given above as the basis for the decision. However, you have been given
the freedom to combine the positions if you think it necessary to present
the best option.
　　You are to decide which position you would take on this issue. Be sure
to give two reasons for your point of view.
　　Next, work with six members of your class as a committee. Hear the
ideas and opinions of all the members of the committee. Try to develop a
consensus opinion among the committee members.

QUESTIONS:
1.　What is the issue here?
2.　Why do those who uphold the first position think that the book should
　　be purged from the library shelf?
3.　Why do those who uphold the second position think the book should
　　be read?
4.　What does the word "censorship" mean?
5.　Can you think of a time when it may be proper to censor a book or
　　information?

6. An argument for purging this book from the school library could be that the book would fall into the hands of a younger brother or sister. The younger sibling could read the book and suffer psychological trauma. What is your position on this argument?

7. Some colleges and universities have refused to allow controversial people to appear and speak on their campuses. Is this censorship of ideas? Should people be prevented from speaking at universities?

EXTENSION:

Mentioning the word "censorship" can bring forth a variety of opinions and an equal number of retorts. Sometimes the arguments are well developed and presented while other times, the arguments are based more on emotions.

Several additional issues should be considered when discussing censorship:

1. Do news organizations have an obligation to withhold information if requested to by the government? Consider the following example: A reporter uncovers the fact that his government is negotiating from a position which is counter to previously expounded philosophy and intentions. A government spokesman asks the reporter not to report the story because the negotiations are at a delicate point and much is at stake. Should this reporter withhold the story?

2. Obviously not all information is made available to the public at large. For one, who would have enough time to read or comprehend the information? Assume that you are the spokesperson for the President. How would you determine what information to give the press and what information to withhold?

The topic of censorship would make an excellent project topic for an entire class. Among the topics to be considered would be:

1. Is censorship necessary?
2. When might it be utilized?
3. Is there a difference between censorship and withholding information?
4. Would it be possible to arrange a debate between those who might favor censorship concerning issues and others who would be against censorship involving the same issues?

Moral Foundations

Moral philosophy represents an entirely different entity than the empirical facts of scientific enquiry. Although morality is interpersonal, it can be objective. "Moral facts" are relational facts about reasons for actions and about the acceptance of certain morally defined social conventions which benefit humans in their social interactions. Thus, as pointed out in our first essay, there will always remain a subjective quality to our moral reconsiderations.

In our effort to explain and understand our moral foundations, there are two considerations which we need to take into account when defining the concept of "morality." First, we need to think functionally about moral judgments. Some moral principles and their resultant actions will hold by virtue of other facts. A behavior may be wrong because of some other features it has; for instance, the behavior may cause needless suffering to ourselves or others or it may betray the trust of a friend. The moral features of a behavior are not independent of other features of the act, but are implied by it. Our question is, "how is 'ought' related to 'is'?", or "how is 'value' related to 'fact'?" In part, the answer will be discovered in the effects of the behavior on human beings, oneself, and others.

This brings up a second consideration. How does one define the concept of morality, the moral point of view, anyway? Morality is intrinsically related to the value or preciousness of persons and other living things. That is, we define certain behaviors as moral or immoral by the effects these behaviors have on persons and these effects in turn assist us in formulating our conception of morality.

What we must understand is that your value as a human being generates a moral claim on my behavior (actions) toward you; because of your value, others (myself included) ought to behave toward you in certain ways. We define these ways in moral terminology. Also, my value is expressed in how I am best off behaving, in the kind of behavior that should flow from a being with my value, in how that value is maintained in my behavior. My value tells you what kind of behavior ought to flow from me; your value tells me what behavior should flow toward you. We are creatures of intrinsic value and our value manifests itself toward other persons in an action of push and pull.

Kurt Baier, in his book, *The Moral Point Of View*, prefers to define the idea of human value, the point of view of morality, in terms of universal human equality and justice. Again, the foundation of these moral concepts lies in the fact of intrinsic human value and is, in part, defined because of its function in promoting this value among other sentient beings.

If a person understands his or her own intrinsic worth, then this worth ought to lead (push) this person to behave toward others in morally consistent ways. As was earlier stated, one's understanding of his or her own value fixes what behavior should flow from that person. In like manner, your value and my understanding of your worth pulls morally consistent behaviors from me to you. Ethics is harmonious when the push and pull are equal— when the person's own value leads him or her to behave toward another as the value of that other requires. This is the bottom line in morality.

Yet, such an activity toward self and toward others is never guaranteed. Our vision may fail. The skeptic may question the relationship between fact and value which we have just outlined. The skeptic may deny the existence of value, intrinsic value, in life and that this value requires us to behave in ways which we have described as "moral." If this is the case, there is very little that we can do except reason with the skeptic. Of course, this may not work either, for the person, if s/he is consistent, will even deny the foundation of any knowledge whatsoever, making explanation and understanding impossible.

One way of understanding the concept of value in the relationships of sentient beings is to provide an analytical breakdown of the concept of "self-interest." At the risk of oversimplification, this analysis should make clear the human connections which reveal the meaning attached to the words "moral" and "value."

SELF-INTEREST

1.	Selfish - interest	"Me First/You Not At All"
2.	Selfcentered - interest	"Me First/You Second"
3.	Unselfish - interest	"You First/Me Second"
4.	Selfless - interest	"You First/Me Not At All"

In this essay we have maintained that life in general, and human life in particular, has intrinsic value for no other reason than its existence. We have also said that the concept of moral value is derived from this fact about sentient beings; that morality takes its meaning in both a functional (its effect on persons) and an organic fashion (the concepts defining this cause/effect relationship).

The above chart makes it clear that only #2, Selfcentered - interest and #3, Unselfish - interest, have any possibility of being definitive of the point of view of morality. #1, Selfish - interest, cannot be moral because it denies the intrinsic worth of other sentient beings. #4, Selfless - interest, appears to be the highest idea of morality that can be conceived because it involves the sacrifice of the "self" for other living beings. This conception of morality has a basic fault—it denies the intrinsic worth of the person performing the behavior. The action of the person may indeed appear to be moral, for example, the saving of a life. But if the person loses his or her life in saving another, he or she has denied the fundamental worth of the self, a denial which cannot possibly be moral.

Only #2, Selfcentered - interest, and #3, Unselfish - interest, stand a chance at being moral. They both recognize the value and worth of other living beings and they both recognize the value and worth of the self who is performing the behaviors. The only difference is place of order — either others are second and self, first; or self is second and others are first.

We have earlier suggested that life can become morally harmonious when the moral push is at least as great as the pull, when the person's own value leads him or her to behave toward another as the value of that other requires. Thus, do we value self first and permit this valuing to aid our valuing of others; or do we value others first because we value ourselves? This is a tough question.

The answer lies before us. It is found in the *harmonious* relationship of push and pull. That is, somewhere between Selfcentered - interest and Unselfish - interest lies the moral equilibrium which we are seeking. Although never guaranteed, the consideration of self and the consideration of others ought to become a dual focus of the moral personality.

In the next essay, Glaucon will ask us for reasons for being moral when morality is unnecessary or when we can be immoral and not get caught at it. When we are faced with the choice between being moral and being immoral, we are confronted with perhaps the most severe challenge to human moral life. To say that life would be better if I were moral just will not always work. Sometimes acting in rational self-interest appears to be best for me, even if it hurts someone else. The answer cannot be found in pitting morality against rational self-interest. Rather, as we read and contemplate this question in the next essay, we should give serious thought to the idea of "intrinsic value." The answer to Glaucon's question is to be found in this concept.

The basic dimension of value is one that underlies and generates our own value ranking. We do not have value for some other purpose, effects, or consequences. Our value is not instrumental, but rather it is value in itself, apart from these further consequences and connections. The chain of being valuable must terminate in something that is valuable in itself; otherwise value could not get started, value would be without foundation. When we begin with the belief that life has intrinsic value, we end there as well. That we seek the foundation of moral values assumes that life has value. This value assumption motivates us to seek foundations, explanations, and under-standings. We are not in a position to question it. We end as we began.

7

CONCEPTUAL SCHEME THREE: VALUES/MORAL THINKING

GOALS AND OBJECTIVES

SCHEMATIC GOAL:

Students will formulate a criteria for evaluating personal, societal, and universal moral values.

More than anything else, the values held by individuals represent dispositions to act in certain ways, ways that can be observed by other people. Defined in this way, values are tendencies in people to devote their resources to the attainment of goals which they consider important. These goals may be personally or socially important.

Also, individuals usually consider their values to be beneficial to them: they will either be good ways of expending their resources of time, money, and energy; or they will tend to make life better than alternative choices which they are free to make. Thus, values reflect human preferences and recommend activities that are worth pursuing.

Values need to be distinguished from attitudes. They represent an internalized continuum of:

interests,
appreciations, and
attitudes.

Thus, values—because they include all three of these characteristics—are more deeply internalized than mere attitudes and thus affect entire ways of life.

For example, in a typical classroom discussion students will, at the outset, simply listen to the positions being outlined and the arguments being presented. They may not form a pro or con opinion until after they have studied the issues very carefully. As they develop an INTEREST in the discussion and are stimulated to make responses, the students will display a willingness to listen and to read further about the subject. Eventually, they will begin to put their own opinions about the subject under scrutiny. By this time some of the students will begin giving opinions and stating strong preferences. These statements will be full of emotional overtones indicating APPRECIATION for their own views and a dislike for the views of others. As they support or justify their positions even further, strong ATTITUDES will be evident in the give and take of argumentation. Taken together, these interests, appreciations, and attitudes indicate a developing set of strong values.

But a value is not merely an attitude. Attitudes are directional. They have the benefit of preparing one to be motivated toward certain courses of action. The problem is that attitudes are irrational. They are full of feeling and represent predispositions to REACT, not act, in certain ways. Attitudes are emotions that have not been brought into the full light of reason.

To distinguish values from attitudes is not an easy task. For many there is no perceivable difference: both are deeply internalized emotions that have the tendency to be fickle and change with the mood of the individual. But both values and attitudes are more stable than simple tastes and preferences. They are more deeply internalized and conceptualized.

Values represent a set of norms which is more deeply internalized than interests, appreciations, or attitudes taken singularly. Actually, values contain these three properties. Attitudes do not. Attitudes contain the properties of interests and appreciations, but not values. Thus, the articulation of a set of values logically implies having an interest in, an appreciation of, and attitudes for the set of behaviors defined.

Values may be distinguished from attitudes in another and probably more important manner. Whereas attitudes are purely affective and reveal strong emotional overtones, values have the additional traits of being both developmental (see Kolberg and Piaget), and of having the possibility of being guided by reason.

Thus, values represent a certain level of both affective and cognitive development among human beings as well as an intentional effort on the part of many to give values the aid of their best reasoning. As adults, we can intellectualize our values. Many of our very best students have similar abilities. Values can be stated as PRESCRIPTIONS to more worthwhile endeavors. Values can be defended logically. Values can also be supported by facts about human societal living.

It is no longer the case that values have to be classified as so utterly subjective that there is no hope of giving them objective status. If one is dedicated to following rational procedures, then a measure of objectivity can be found.

SOME CLASSROOM IMPLICATIONS...

Both cognitive and affective learning should be pursued in the classroom. One of these areas ought not be promoted over the other. Although state and local testing procedures normally emphasize the cognitive domain of knowledges, teachers should take very seriously the responsibility of emphasizing both knowledges and understandings. **An understanding is a fact in which the conceptual and value-implications have been illuminated and explored.**

If a teacher focuses only on the affective, the classroom environment will have a strong tendency to overstate one person's ideas and answers. There probably will be no correct or incorrect answers. Each student's ideas are as good as the next. Here classroom FORM conquers MATTER, and method wins out over the attainment of knowledges and understanding.

Why can't teachers evaluate ideas?

Why can't teachers teach the evaluational process?

Can a person be right all the time?

Isn't it unrealistic to fear that to question a student's responses damages the student's self-esteem or calls into question the student's societal background? Self-esteem is never built upon a foundation that promotes falsehood or on a methodology that neglects the real world.

Of course, if only facts are emphasized in the classroom, the outcome can be sterile and boring. A balanced approach will bring both facts and values into focus. Knowledges have the function of assisting reason by shoring up values and supporting actions. They can provide a touch of reality to one's interests and attitudes. Along with reason, knowledge gives the dimension of logical consistency to value judgments and decision making. On the other hand, values can give depth and an introspective quality to the search for knowledge.

Facts themselves may ultimately be value free, but the method that discovers them is not. As long as teachers speak and students respond, there will be values in the public school classroom. Values form the sieve through which is poured the facts for one's evaluation and interpretation.

VALUE CHOICES...

We live during a time in which values matter. Value choices can no longer be taken for granted. This is a period in which our values are under strain. There is a CONFLICT going on in our world, in our classrooms. It is a conflict in the minds of individuals about basic value choices.

All of our values are being challenged. Basic transformations of the quantity, quality, and texture of human life are now underway. Many vital choices of value are being made. But how can a person make such vital choices? Are not the values one already holds the rational determinants of one's present decisions? How does one break out of this mold? Can a person break the bonds of environmental influence? If one must choose new values or change existing ones, where does a person begin? How does one select them?

Humanly speaking, all one can do is question the soundness (the validity) of the values to which one now subscribes. The tug and pull of social gravity (ethnocentrism) is very real. One cannot step outside of one's cultural adaptations and start life anew. Would a person actually want to do this anyway? New ideas and innovative processes are fundamentally constructed from the living tree of culture. The acculturation process has provided humans with a set of ready-made values—effective or ineffective, good or bad. Although these values are fluid, they tend to become fixed in certain individuals. Every new experience and idea can add to these values. The discovery of new information can clarify existing values and help humans evaluate their effectiveness in day-to-day living.

The teacher's task is to re-think existing values in the light of new experiences and new understandings. The teacher should help students in this re-thinking process. This activity can be divided into three components:

1. One first needs to identify, interpret, and seek out the implications of one's existing set of values;

2. Then one needs to isolate those factors which tend to preserve these values and those factors which tend to undermine these values; and

3. Finally, one needs to develop a technique for evaluating the validity of these values and the characteristics of the situations that tend to preserve or undermine them.

The re-thinking process is a selective task. With the aid of human reason one makes an effort to identify certain values with the idea that some will be discarded for lack of factual and/or rational support, while others will be kept because they are supported both factually and rationally.

Of course this process will not work if one does not have the proper MOTIVATION to:

seek out,
understand,
evaluate, and finally
modify one's values.

It will make little difference to anyone else if, after this process has been completed, one does not act on the basis of the values which have been so energetically defined and rationally supported.

SUGGESTED CURRICULUM OUTLINE...

In the following three units your students will be given the opportunity to complete this task. Additionally, one of the major problems you will confront in the discussion of values is their seeming arbitrariness. At the end of this chapter this fundamental problem is outlined in detail.

Below is presented a suggested curriculum outline which will help students deal with the topics and ideas covered in this chapter.

I.   UNIT ONE: Values and Normative Behavior
UNIT OBJECTIVE:
Students will distinguish between personal, societal, and universal (global) values.
TASK DESCRIPTIONS:
A.   KNOWLEDGES
Students will. . .
1.   Identify their personal values.
2.   Identify the values exhibited by their society's major social institutions.
3.   Be able to recognize value dilemma situations when they occur.
4.   Discuss value dilemma situations with the class.
5.   Restate value preferences in a consistent manner.
6.   Consistently apply value choices in their social behaviors.

B. CONCEPTS
Students will define the following terms:
1. Value
2. Value preference
3. Value choice
4. Value decision
5. Value dilemma

C. VALUES
Students will. . .
1. Demonstrate a willingness to share personal value preferences.
2. Demonstrate a tolerance for the developing values of others.
3. Tell why values ought to be clarified and restated.
4. Show a willingness to express personal values in conflicting situations.
5. Demonstrate patience and empathy as classmates struggle to clarify their values.
6. Demonstrate consistency in making decisions.

D. SKILLS
Students will. . .
1. Make inferences from one value dilemma to similar social situations.
2. Identify the implications of their value choices.
3. Demonstrate consistency in value preferences.
4. Illustrate value implications by writing scenarios.
5. Consistently apply values in different situations.
6. Evaluate the values of their society's major institutions.
7. Distinguish between a personal value and a social value.
8. From personal and societal values, choose those elements which make up global or universal values.
9. Construct universal moral principles, applicable to all human beings.

II. UNIT TWO: Morality
UNIT OBJECTIVE:
Students will identify morals as a distinct set of values and seek their rational support.
TASK DESCRIPTIONS:
A. KNOWLEDGES

Students will...
1.   Distinguish a moral principle from a personal or social value.
2.   Name the social and logical limits of a moral principle.
3.   State the position of moral subjectivism.
4.   Differentiate between the subjective and objective traits of moral reasoning.
5.   Identify reasons for adopting one conception of morality over another.
6.   Tell why a person should justify her/his moral values.

B.   CONCEPTS
Students will define the following terms:
1.   Moral subjectivism
2.   Moral relativism
3.   Moral absolutism
4.   Moral universalism
5.   A principle
6.   A rule
7.   Reasoning
8.   Ethnocentrism
9.   Justification
10.   Moral skepticism

C.   VALUES
Students will. . .
1.   Tell why moral reasoning is socially important.
2.   Demonstrate an effort to achieve moral consistency.
3.   Tell why personal values ought to be evaluated.
4.   Apply moral principles in situations of conflicting interests.

D.   SKILLS
Students will. . .
1.   Identify moral-conflict situations.
2.   Write a set of moral principles.
3.   Locate and present evidence to support moral principles.
4.   Analyze the moral statements of others.
5.   Restate another's moral principles in one's own words.
6.   Identify similarities and differences among conflicting moral choices.
7.   Give a critical evaluation of the moral actions of others.
8.   Explain why a particular conception of morality can help resolve problems when interests conflict.
9.   Restate the problem of moral skepticism in their own words.
10.   Apply previously learned ideas from this unit to resolve the problem of moral skepticism.

III. UNIT THREE: Principles of Social and Political Thought
UNIT OBJECTIVE:
Students will assess the value of the principles governing the democratic state.
TASK DESCRIPTIONS:
A. KNOWLEDGES
Students will. . .
1. Identify types of social regulation in a democratic society.
2. Identify the legal procedures used in a democratic society.
3. Discuss the principles embodied in the Bill of Rights.
4. Tell why a democratic society ought to tolerate some social and political deviance.
5. Restate in their own words the problem of federalism and states' rights.
6. Tell why voting is an important function in a democratic society.
B. CONCEPTS
Students will define the following terms:
1. Law
2. Justice
3. Property rights
4. Equality
5. Freedom
6. Human rights
7. Democracy
8. The state
9. Sovereignty
10. Authority
11. States' rights
12. Federalism
C. VALUES
Students will. . .
1. Demonstrate a willingness to discuss the principles of the democratic state.
2. Tell why one needs to clarify the major principles of a democratic state.
3. Demonstrate tolerance for the variety of people, beliefs, and customs which exist in a democratic society.
4. Show a willingness to evaluate the moral concepts which are supportive of the democratic process.

       4.   Show a willingness to evaluate the moral concepts which are supportive of the democratic process.

D.   SKILLS. . .

Students will. . .

       1.   State the requirements they think are necessary for the creation of an international democratic society.

       2.   Develop (write) criteria for establishing moral relationships between different countries.

       3.   Discuss the scope and limits of international law.

       4.   Appraise the need for and the validity of a "world state."

       5.   Compare the quest for civil rights by black people in the United States during the 1950's and 1960's with the arguments for women's rights in the 1970's.

Telling "Right" from "Wrong"

The field of moral values is often called "ethics." Traditionally, ethics has been preoccupied with defining what is good or what is right. The assumption is that GOOD and RIGHT are constants in nature discernible to all who look. What has been overlooked is HOW one comes to distinguish between good and evil, right and wrong. This problem can best be understood as an answer to a series of questions:

1. Where there are conflicting choices open to a person, which alternative should one choose?

2. Often one is torn between conflicting loyalties: to which ought one adhere?

3. Must all choices between right and wrong be arbitrary?

4. Must the decision be left to subjective preference when making value choices?

5. Must one conclude, that in ethics, anything goes?

6. In ethics, is there an objective standard to which one can appeal for guidance?

These are fundamental questions. Failure to answer them is surely a basic source of social confusion. They represent the plaguing problems associated with moral values.

Generally, there have been two approaches to answering these questions. One approach is that of MORAL SKEPTICISM. This position has taken several different forms and emphasizes the subjective and arbitrary nature of moral values.

The second approach has been the various attempts to avoid the skeptical position. In this domain there have been many positions defined and defended. Here we will present the rudiments of a position, which for lack of a better name, is called the position of "moral validation." MORAL VALIDATION is the attempt to provide a measure of objectivity in ethical decision-making via sound methods of reasoning.

As a teacher, one must come to terms with the central problem of ethics: Are all of one's choices merely arbitrary and, therefore, always right? Does one have any valid way of saying that some choices are wrong, and therefore, on moral grounds, ought to be avoided?

During the classroom process of values' clarification, the role of the teacher is that of a facilitator. The quest is to sort out and understand one's own values, and to examine how one has made some choices.

But as one begins to probe into the present and future areas of choosing values, questions of how to make better and more efficient choices are bound to arise. Questions of how to make society and the world better places in which to live will arise in the context of classroom discussions. When this occurs, students will begin to state their value preferences. Interests, feelings, and attitudes will be involved as the class ponders moral dilemmas.

During these discussions, the question of moral standards or moral criteria ought to be raised. For students, the important point is how one should define the basic ingredients of THE MORAL POINT OF VIEW. Once the question of criteria has been raised, the class is ready to tackle the problem of skepticism versus objectivism in moral value theory. An understanding of this problem will greatly illuminate and enhance classroom discussions. REMEMBER, there are no easy answers, and, in the final analysis, many will not agree. The challenge is to present one's position clearly and consistently, and to give solid support for each step taken.

A.   WHAT ARE THE SOURCES OF MORAL SKEPTICISM?
    1.   Are morals culturally relative?
        From cultural anthropology one learns that the mores of a society can make anything right; the standards of good and right are in the mores/customs/traditions of a societal group. The essence of this position is that two people may assert CONTRADICTORY moral views without either person being mistaken. How is this possible? "Right" for one person, defined by a definite set of mores, is not necessarily "right" for those with differing mores. This is the position of ethical relativism.

        The positive side of this position is that it promotes respect and tolerance for the practices of different cultures around the world, or next door. The negative side of this position is that it tells us that there are no transcultural standards by which any particular society can be judged.

2. Are morals subjective and tied to one's interests?
    There are many forms of ETHICAL SUBJECTIVITY. Here we
    will present the "Interest Theory of Value." Basically, this theory
    says that a moral judgment expresses the fact that the author of
    such a judgment has a particular preference (which is defined as
    a feeling of approval or an interest) about a course of action, and
    that the judgment gives information about this person's interests.
    Outline: The Interest Theory of Value
    (i)   Absolute claims of laws and codes must be tested
           against human needs and desires.
    (ii)   There are a variety of feelings related to our gratifica-
           tion of these needs and desires.
    (iii) These feelings do not cause our desires or interests.
    (iv)   Thus, it is interest which is the original source and
           constant feature of all value.
    (v)   This is interpreted to mean:
           "X is valuable = interest is taken in X."
           Thus, anything acquires value when an interest is taken
           in it.

3. Are morals related to emotions?
    The emotive theory is a product of Twentieth Century analytic
    philosophy. Unable to verify value judgments scientifically, an-
    alytic philosophers rejected their claim to cognition and assigned
    to them the status of an emotional expression. Such philosophers
    hold that there is an innate difference between facts and values.
    They express the nature of the difference in such terminology as
    fact/value, description/prescription, and cognitive/emotive.
    MEANING is only assigned to facts which are themselves obser-
    vational statements or logically consistent inferences made from
    observational statements.

    For example, the statement, "I love my wife" would not be
    a statement of fact, but a statement of emotion. "I love my wife"
    may be a statement of fact if and only if I act in certain ways
    (observable to others) toward my wife.

    According to the emotive theory, statements of value are not
    used to report facts. They are used to create an influence. Their
    origin is in one's feelings and their intent is to recommend, to
    alter interests, to prescribe different ways of behaving. All value
    statements are limited, by this theory, to affective responses.
    They are purely and simply emotive.

For example, if I say to my wife, "I love you," the sentence, "I love you" is not a statement of fact but a quasi-imperative statement whose purpose is to influence and modify a course of action or a way of thinking. It has no cognitive status whatsoever.

B.   IS THERE AN ALTERNATIVE TO MORAL SKEPTICISM?

When one deliberates in a state of moral perplexity, the key question is, "What ought I to do?" When one has, for some reason, discovered that personal goals are no longer worthwhile, that one's standards are no longer useful, one feels obligated to discover why this is the case. One is challenged to suspend the principles by which one has heretofore been guided, to re-examine them, to modify them, and, if need be, to abandon them for newer ones.

This process begins with clarifying (sorting out and understanding) the values one now holds dear; then comes the process of validation. MORAL VALIDATION includes the following:

1.   Stating a general moral criterion (principle) that can serve all people as a guide for settling conflicting interests.

2.   The separation of principles from rules. A principle is a generalized truth which is the foundation of other truths.

   Principles explain how other things act. They represent a method of operation.

   On the other hand, rules are more particular statements of what to do and what not to do; they are limited to individual cases.

   A moral principle will have a universal quality; it will be alike for all people. It will express such ideas as equality, nondiscrimination, and unselfishness.

   A rule, either societal or personal—to be called moral—must be logically consistent with the more generally operational moral principle.

3.   Giving reasons for preferring one moral principle over another. Such reasons provide an objective cognitive basis for calling moral principles "justified" or "unjustified," "validated" or "invalid."

   Moral principles will be generally PRESCRIPTIVE rather than descriptive. But they will have their roots firmly anchored in facts about human societal living. These principles will not be confirmed or denied as are true or false descriptive statements about matters of fact. Rather, they will represent consistent prescriptions on how to live in order to maximize the quality of human life.

4. Assigning objective status to personal and societal values on the basis of whether they are consistent with the more generalized and rationally supported moral criterion:

    MORAL HIERARCHY
    a. Moral Principles
        (i)   Universal
        (ii) Egalitarian
    b. Social rules, laws, etc.
    c. Personal values

When conceived in this way, moral reasoning becomes a SCIENCE OF VALUES. This science of values:

a. Approaches moral life as a natural and social phenomenon rather than something supernatural or purely emotional;

b. Attempts to understand values in terms of general principles which reflect the closely examined facts of human societal living. (NOTE: One can show that all humans have basically the same needs and that there are rationally efficient ways of handling these needs in a world growing closer together each day.);

c. Is both descriptive and prescriptive in that it gives an account of human experience and then recommends ways of living that, on principle, ought to be undertaken; and

d. Takes into account the only principle of objectivity in science, the principle of RECONSIDERATION.

It all depends on how one carries out the task of moral decision-making. If one is willing to rethink or reconsider any idea, fact, or value in the light of new knowledges and fresh understandings, then one will have a better chance of being objective in one's moral deliberations and actions.

Snake Eyes

PROBLEM:

A judge is presiding over the trial of the State versus The Wholiness Church. The Wholiness Church handles snakes as a part of its worship service. The State is seeking to stop this practice. Meanwhile, the defense argues the prosecution is violating the separation of Church and State which is guaranteed by the Bill of Rights under the Constitution.

The prosecution argues that the snake-handling-church puts its own members and other citizens who attend the church in a dangerous position. Individuals who handle poisonous snakes during the worship service could be bitten and unable to get to a hospital or choose not to go. The state further argues that taking children to this worship service could prove psychologically harmful to them. A child could be psychologically abused if not accidentally bitten by a snake, and killed. Outside the church, a child's peers could judge the child as bizarre for attending the church. A peer isolation could occur which could make the child feel that s/he is not liked. Such children could suffer developmental trauma.

The church defense argues that their command to handle snakes comes from the Bible. They cite Chapter Sixteen, Verses 17-18 of the Book of Mark as their source:

> And these signs shall follow them that believe; In my name shall they cast out devils; they shall speak with new tongues. They shall take up serpents and if they drink any deadly thing, it shall not hurt them; they shall lay hands on the sick and they shall recover.

The church considers the Bible to be the supreme lawgiver. It is the word of God and should be obeyed. Should a snake bite someone, it is considered to be God's Will. In answering the point that snake handling in church is psychologically harmful to children, the church's lawyer responds, "How could God's Word be psychologically harmful? God's Word conquers all and must be obeyed. In addition the children are not allowed to handle and are kept away from the snakes until they reach adulthood."

Finally the church defense appeals to The United States Bill of Rights under Article 1: "Congress shall make no law respecting an establishment of religion, or prohibiting the free exercise thereof..." It would appear to be a violation of Article 1 if the State was to attempt to outlaw the handling of snakes within a worship service. The state has no right to interfere with what goes on inside a church service. At this point the defense rests its case.

ACTIVITY:

Suppose you were the judge. It is up to you to make a decision as to the legality of the poisonous snake-handling service. While the decision is important, the reasons you give to justify your decision will be critical. Decide what you feel to be the best possible decision in this particular case and give three reasons in support of your decision.

QUESTIONS:

1. What is the state's position?
2. What is the position of the church?
3. Why is the state concerned about children who simply observe the handling of snakes within the service?
4. What is a "church?"
5. How does a church service differ from a religion?
6. Suppose the church offered willing human sacrifices. Would this practice be guaranteed within the Bill of Rights? Explain.
7. The state also guarantees a right to an education for each child. A church has decided it will educate its own children separate from the schools of the state. What could be some possible disputes between the two?

EXTENSION:

The issue concerning the separation of Church and State is one which is receiving more and more attention. What is the role of the state in the possible regulation of what can be done in the name of religion? Is there always a clear division between a church as a religious institution and as a business (i.e., T.V. evangelists)?

Another issue concerns church schools which may fail, although it must be noted that many do not, to teach academic skills which will allow a pupil to compete in advanced study or a workplace. For some schools the Bible and its interpretation represents all the education which is needed. In this case, is the state responsible for intervening in the schooling of these children; and if so, in what manner?

Finally, the previous problem sheet offers a great opportunity for a mock trial. Divide the students into three groups. One group will represent the church while another will represent the state. The third group will be the jury. Have the students organize a trial concerning the issue. If possible, seek actual legal advice from individuals within the community. Seek the input of scholars, church and lay persons. This will help add depth to the activity.

PHILOSOPHICAL PROBLEM SHEET #13

Hot Possibilities in Lizard Lick

PROBLEM:

A crime was committed in the large city of Lizard Lick. The police think they know who committed the crime. However, they have been unable to find enough evidence which would stand up in court. In addition, the individual thought to be guilty has left the country. His whereabouts are unknown.

The area where the murder occurred is a poor community consisting of many nationalities. The needs of this community have been neglected for years. Bill Malory, the man who was killed, had worked his way up from the poorest area of the community to become a council member and a political power in the city. Mr. Malory had worked hard to establish programs within the community. He was granted a large sum of money to bring the recreational program of this community up to a level with all other areas. The people in the community had contributed to a fund to show they too would help support Malory's programs. Now with the murder, the community has become quite tense. The police, who were highly thought of in the community, are under attack for failure to apprehend the criminal. The general feeling in the community is like a ticking bomb waiting to go off!

The police chief, Stu Tippett, and two council members, Candice Devine and Robert Sudden realized that something had to be done. All three knew the situation could only relax after the murderer was found. Knowing that the person they suspected could not be found or prosecuted, they decided to find someone who ''committed'' the crime. They based their decision on the concept of providing the ''greatest good for the greatest number.'' By finding someone who could be accused and convicted of committing the crime, the community's tense attitude might relax without public disturbances. This conviction would also provide time for the city to appropriate funds and begin building the recreational facilities. The community would then feel more a part of the city. This feeling of belonging would benefit the city as a whole. Finally, Mr. Tippett, Ms. Devine, and Mr. Sudden believe that finding someone to stand trial would restore the reputation of the police in the community.

The police were able to find someone who was a derelict, living in old buildings. They accused this person of committing the murder. This individual had no history of violent crimes. However, he had been overheard saying he hated Mr. Malory and would like to see him dead. By lining up witnesses and using good arguments, the prosecution was able to obtain a guilty verdict. The city was able to continue the policies of Malory and to help bring the community more into the mainstream of the city. The police were looked upon more favorably within the community which pleased Mr. Tippett, Ms. Devine, and Mr. Sudden. The community's pride was increased by their new buildings. In turn, they began to fix up other buildings. Much of this eventual good was attributed to the conviction.

ACTIVITY:

Suppose you live in this community and have just found out about the framing of the derelict. You have also seen the new pride in your community and would hate to see all of this good broken down. You have three choices:

1.   Go public and tell all you know concerning the framing of this individual. Problems could arise which could possibly break down trust towards the governing power in the city. The neighborhood could get tense again.
2.   You could remain quiet, but agree to yourself that this innocent person is paying for a crime he did not commit. The greater gains of the community and the city are worth the suffering of one individual.
3.   You could give an anonymous tip to a newspaper. Perhaps if they felt the issue deserved special merit, they would launch an investigation.

   State your choice and give two reasons for it. State your reasons for refusing the other choices.

QUESTIONS:

1.   What position did Mr. Malory play in the community?
2.   Why were the police unable to arrest the individual they believed had committed the crime?
3.   What did the police decide to do to calm the potentially dangerous situation?
4.   If the situation had not calmed down, what might have been some consequences?
5.   How did the decision by Mr. Tippett, Ms. Devine, and Mr. Sudden, and the subsequent conviction of the derelict affect the community?
6.   Do the rights of individuals come before the needs of a community?

Can you give examples?
7. What are some examples of situations where some people had more "rights" than others?

EXTENSION:

Of critical importance in this activity is the issue of providing the greatest good for the greatest number, or utilitarianism. Much of our government and, indeed, our workplace and lives utilize this principle. In most cases, this issue does not involve moral dilemmas.

However, in the above example, the rights of an individual were sacrificed for the betterment of the whole. Can one be justified in sacrificing the rights of one for the betterment of many? Several issues should be addressed.

1. Would a utilitarian ever consider the possibility of sacrificing the rights of an individual to benefit the majority? Even in one case, if one person's rights were violated, could the majority have any gain? It could be argued that providing the greatest good for the greatest number involves the maintenance of individual rights.

2. If one would argue that it might be possible to sacrifice the rights of an individual or group to benefit the majority, how many would justify the majority in a particular situation? Ten? A hundred? One thousand? Is it possible to assign a number when an individual or group of individuals will receive a reduction or loss of rights in order to benefit the majority?

3. John Rawls has argued that rights or what is good should be assigned based on a "veil of ignorance." One assumes the position that one does not know into what part or aspect of a society one will be born. One could be born with a "silver spoon" or in the depths of poverty. Based on this condition, what rules or principles should be established? In this case, if one would not be a majority representative, would one vote to allow the greatest good for the greatest number?

Clearly, this is a most complex issue (as are most philosophical issues!). The above is incomplete and is only meant to whet the appetite. Perhaps some students would be interested in creating a list of issues where utilitarian principles are utilized. This list could then be prioritized and students could investigate the concepts, attitudes, and applications important to each one.

PHILOSOPHICAL PROBLEM SHEET #14

Up from the Slumber

PROBLEM:

Smithville is a small town located in a rural section of a state. Until recently, the town maintained its sleepy image. A few months ago, an abortion clinic moved into the town. Some people want it removed from town. Others feel the clinic should be allowed to stay. The town council has jurisdiction over matters such as this. The council has decided it will hear arguments from the citizens of the town in order to clarify the issues within the various positions on abortion. From these arguments, the council will determine the fate of the clinic. Four positions were presented:

1.   The first position states that abortion is wrong under all circumstances. This includes fetuses which have been diagnosed through modern medical techniques as severely handicapped. This also includes women who have been raped and/or whose lives would be threatened by having a child. There is absolutely no justification for abortion.

2.   The second position states abortion should be granted only under four possibilities:
    a.   Through the use of advanced medical techniques, a fetus is found to be severely handicapped. This position maintains it unfair for the family and for the handicapped individual to be forced into this world,
    b.   When the pregnant woman was raped,
    c.   When a fetus was conceived through forced incest, and
    d.   When carrying the fetus would endanger the life of the woman.

3.   The third position argues abortion should be allowed in all the above cases and also when psychological damage could result for the mother carrying the fetus. An example would be a mother who felt she was emotionally unable to carry this fetus until birth. Still another example might be the psychological stress of a young girl carrying the child.

4.   Position four maintains that abortion is accepted under all conditions. A woman has a right to control her body without interference from the town council. The carrying of the fetus is a decision of the mother

and not a right of the fetus. The fetus can therefore be aborted at the mother's discretion. When questioned as to what time the abortion could be performed, the group stated that before the 20th week would be their preference, or until the fetus was unable to live outside the mother's womb.

ACTIVITY:
You have now heard all four positions. As a member of the council, you must help decide what position should be accepted. In order to clarify your position you should rank the choices in order of preference from first choice to last choice. Questions to help you clarify your position follow:
1.   The most preferable policy is:
2.   If challenged to justify this policy I would state the following:
3.   Anticipated positive consequences of this policy are:
4.   Possible negative consequences of this policy are:
5.   My second policy preference is:
6.   My third policy preference is:
7.   My fourth policy preference is:

QUESTIONS:
1.   What does the word abortion mean?
2.   When does an embryo become a fetus?
3.   At what point in time does a human life begin?
4.   At what point in time does a human being begin?
5.   At what point in time does death occur?
6.   Does an unborn fetus have any rights?
7.   Compare ideas and definitions of "human" and "person". Does the definition or ideas about these terms differ?
8.   How might differences in these terms affect considerations on moral issues?

EXTENSION:
This issue has become so highly charged with emotion in our society that it is difficult to handle in the classroom. Among the possibilities are a debate between the members of your class or between proponents from the community. Also, a panel of doctors, lawyers, ministers, students, etc., could be created. Each panel member would explain his or her position in front of the student body. When each panel member had finished, the other panel members could respond and then the audience could ask questions.

PHILOSOPHICAL PROBLEM SHEET #15
Society's Child

PROBLEM:
A group of individuals has become increasingly disenchanted with the present state of society. Its major concern is the lack of moral judgment and action within society. This perceived moral decadence exists from the highest levels of government down to the interactions people have with each other on the street. Recently, the group, Citizens for Moral Lives (CML) bought vast acreage in Canada and decided to set up a new society based on their moral principles.

ACTIVITY:
You are one of the leaders of the group. Your task is to examine and make recommendations to adopt one of the positions presented as the cornerstone of the society. Your choice is to come from the following positions:

Moral Position I: This position maintains the desire to "do one's duty." One shows respect for the laws of society and for those within the society, not for the benefit of the individual but to maintain the given social order for its own sake. One's duty is separate from individual gains. Duty consists of following the laws without thinking of how one will profit from them. As an example, I follow the law concerning the import tax not because I might benefit from the tax but because it is the law and should be followed.

Moral Position II: I will follow the law for fear of being punished. Without a fear of punishment, individuals would freely break the law. Therefore laws should be established and punishment attached to each violation. The justification of this principle would be an individual who violates a rule of law and attempts to avoid the punishment through legal loopholes. This position would stop such actions.

Moral Position III: This position maintains a starting point in rules or expectations. One would seek to treat individuals as an ends rather than a means to an end. As an example, assume that a law was established which violated the rights as established by the Constitution and Bill of Rights. I would then be justified in violating that law if the law violated the rights of other persons. In that sense, I would do what is moral based on defined and determined moral principles, not necessarily the laws.

Moral Position IV: This position maintains that one should do what the majority does and what the majority determines is good. One adopts this position to be pleasing or helpful towards others. The needs of the community will be what one strives to achieve. By acknowledging and adopting the needs of the community and working towards these needs, the community will come together. By doing what the community determines is good, individuals will be working towards the same ends and will prosper.

Moral Position V: This position advocates that the needs of the self must be met before one can consider the needs of others. This does not mean that a person would not consider other persons' needs. One would just attempt to meet one's own needs and then consider helping another. One could perhaps enter into an agreement with another in the community. Perhaps this person would agree to help you if you help this individual. Either way, the needs of the self would be provided for and perhaps the needs of another.

In order for your group to make the very best decision, you decide to discuss each moral position in order to gain a better understanding of the issues. Afterwards, you will rank order the positions from the one you find most appealing down to the least appealing alternative. Give two reasons for your preferred choice and two reasons why the fifth alternative was deemed unacceptable.

State the positions you favor most and least for the community and give two reasons for your most, and two reasons for your least favored positions. Afterwards, you are to decide as a group which position to maintain as the cornerstone of the CML. A key point will be to entertain the ideas of all the members in a group.

QUESTIONS:
1.   What is the major concern of the Citizens for Moral Lives?
2.   What might be some problems with adopting a new code of moral behavior separate from previous codes?

3. Why does society need a moral code to determine proper action?
4. Would the Biblical Scripture, "Do unto others as you would have others do unto you," be a good moral code? Why or why not?
5. How do lawmakers determine whether a law is moral or not?
6. What is the difference between a moral law and a moral principle?
7. Can you give an example of a moral principle?

EXTENSION:
The previous activity is based upon the Stages of Moral Development as developed by Dr. Lawrence Kohlberg of Harvard University. (The positions are not in the order of Kohlberg's stages. The following are Kohlberg's stages of moral development.

Postconventional Level 3 Moral decisions based on shared or shareable standards, rights and duties	Stage 6 Conscience or principle orientation with appeals to ethical universality and consistency. Stage 5 Social contract and interpersonal commitments orientation.
Conventional Level 2 Moral values reside in performing right roles and maintaining conventional order.	Stage 4 Orientation to maintaining authority and social order. Stage 3 Good boy/girl orientation. Conformity to stereotyped cultural images.
Preconventional Level 1 Moral values reside in external events and quasiphysical needs.	Stage 2 Naively egotistic orientation. Right action is instrumentally satisfying. Stage 1 Obedience and punishment orientation. Egocentric deference to a superior power.

Kohlberg's work represents the cornerstone of moral development for many individuals interested in this field. Some studies have attempted to determine what kinds of activities can facilitate moral development in individuals. Briefly, it does appear that allowing and encouraging students to engage in dialogue about moral issues does facilitate moral development. Actually, this is not hard to imagine. If one reads the dialogues of Plato, one notes that Socrates was always attempting to have individuals clarify what they meant concerning a particular position.

A good extension would be to have students research and study what various philosophers have stated concerning the establishment of moral principles as a guide to action. The students would note that various individuals have stated various ideas although each has attempted to define actions which would consist of the moral life.

Another activity would be to read ''Death of Socrates'' or "The Crito". Should Socrates have left Athens instead of dying? What were his reasons for staying? Were these justifiable reasons? This is an excellent and most readable dialogue in which to engage students in defining proper moral action.

Kohlberg's work represents the cornerstone of moral development for many individuals interested in this field. Some studies have attempted to determine what kinds of activities can facilitate moral development in individuals. Briefly, it does appear that allowing and encouraging students to engage in dialogue about moral issues does facilitate moral development. Actually, this is not hard to imagine. If one reads the dialogues of Plato, one notes that Socrates was always attempting to have individuals clarify what they meant concerning a particular position.

A good extension would be to have students research and study what various philosophers have stated concerning the establishment of moral principles as a guide to action. The students would note that various individuals have stated various ideas although each has attempted to define actions which would consist of the moral life.

Another activity would be to read ''Death of Socrates'' or "The Crito". Should Socrates have left Athens instead of dying? What were his reasons for staying? Were these justifiable reasons? This is an excellent and most readable dialogue in which to engage students in defining proper moral action.

PHILOSOPHICAL PROBLEM SHEET #16

Harry's Fate

PROBLEM:

Just recently, a discovery occurred which has scientists baffled. They do not know what to do with what they have discovered!

Bigfoot, an ape-like creature which is reported to roam the wilderness areas of the western United States, has long been considered to be a myth. However, geologists came across such an "animal" while looking for natural gas in this region. The animal had been seriously injured. It was taken to a hospital for medical attention. Several days later they announced the discovery of "an animal with both human and ape-like characteristics."

The ape/man who was named HARRY, has a head shaped like a human head; but he has hair all around it. He also has a human-like face and a beard. Since Harry's age was determined to be about five years, a beard was rare indeed! Harry walks more like a man than an ape. His body is covered with hair, although it is not as thick as that of an ape, but thicker than that of man. Harry is four feet tall, about the size and weight of a five-year-old child.

When Harry was taken from the woods and put into a new environment, he appeared to be nervous and upset. He cried for hours at a time. Gradually, he began to allow human attention. Within two months, he was playing with toys and with his new human friends. Harry appears unable to speak like humans, but he does have a very thorough system of sounds he associates with various objects and desires.

Harry has also exhibited the ability to show affection and emotion. His mental ability resembles that of a four-year-old human child. How much mental ability Harry actually possesses is unknown.

ACTIVITY:

When Harry was first found, the major emphasis was on saving his life. Now that Harry is physically well, decisions need to be made concerning his future. Three scientific organizations have presented their opinion on the "Harry Problem:"

(1) The Scientists For Human Rights feel that Harry should be kept in a zoo. They argue that Harry does not have the physical characteristics of a

human being and, therefore, should not be given the same rights afforded other humans. Harry has hair all over his body like other apes. He cannot talk or communicate like other five-year old humans. Thus, he is a non-human!

This society guarantees certain rights for human members of society (freedom of speech, freedom of religion, freedom of the press, etc.). It would be awkward to grant a nonhuman these rights. It would be almost impossible for Harry to assume the responsibility that goes with such free-doms/rights.

The Scientists For Human Rights advocate a good home for Harry—the zoo! Such a place would provide him health care and comfort. He could live there and enjoy human and nonhuman contact. The zoo could provide him with a wilderness habitat and scientists could go there to study his "animal" behavior.

(2) Another group, Scientists For A Productive Environment, say that Harry should be treated with the same rights and privileges as are granted to human members of our society. Although Harry may LOOK like an ape, he also appears to possess human-like mental and physical characteristics. They claim that if a human possesses a physical or mental handicap (loses an arm or a leg, mental retardation), then this person is not considered to be a nonhuman! This human can still perform and behave like other humans to some degree or another.

Now, Harry shows emotions and affections like a small child. He puts together sounds when he wants certain objects; he cries for affection; he can eat with a spoon. They feel that with enough work and care, Harry will one day be capable of communication on a higher level than that conceivable for an ape.

Rights are not determined for humans by physical characteristics alone. There are mental/emotional and social abilities that must be taken into consideration. This group maintains that Harry should be given a home with intelligent and caring people who can develop his potential and possibilities. This would assist Harry in realizing his rights and aspirations.

(3) The third group, The Scientists For Species Continuation, tells us that Harry should be taken back to the wilderness area where he was first disco-vered and freed. Harry, like other individuals, represents a natural species. He is a product of his biological heredity and natural environment. A particu-

lar environment requires that a species develop certain physical and mental characteristics. For example, a mountain goat has a heavy fur coat and the ability to walk on steep and treacherous mountainsides. Humans also develop certain characteristics consistent with their environment (advanced thinking skills, etc.). Harry's species developed communication skills and a thick body of hair consistent with the demands of the environment.

Removing Harry from his previous environment and placing him in a zoo violates the laws of nature (Harry's need to remain at the level of his physical and mental development; he is suited for survival in this environment). Harry's right is the right to be free. It is the right to be separate from human influence.

These and other groups interested in Harry's fate have been unable to reach a decision over what to do with Harry. Recently they met and decided that an independent group should be chosen from various professional positions and attempt to reach a decision concerning Harry. You have been selected to be in the independent group. Each member of the group is to study the positions and decide the best possible fate for Harry. When you make your decision, give two reasons that will justify it. Next, give one or two reasons why the other positions are unacceptable.

QUESTIONS:
1. What was the physical make-up of Harry?
2. What mental abilities was Harry capable of exhibiting?
3. Which of the scientific groups considered human rights to be specifically related to mental characteristics? How did they argue their position?
4. Which of the scientific groups considered human rights to be specifically related to physical characteristics? How did they argue their position?
5. What rights should all "humans" have?
6. How would you explain to a "being" from another planet the variation in human rights on our planet (from nation to nation, etc.)?
7. Suppose society grants rights to individuals based on their ability to think and reason; would a computer be granted rights? Why? Why not?
8. Consider the rights that you exercise as a human being (name them); what is the basis of these rights? Can you state this as a generality—for all people alike?

EXTENSION:
This activity can be used in conjunction with the position outlined on animal rights. These are several areas which may be emphasized within this activity:
1. Is the issue of rights based on intelligence or physical appearance? Assume that Harry could develop and exhibit the general intelligence of a ten-year-old. Should Harry therefore be granted the same rights as a human being? We, as a society, do not revoke rights from physically or mentally disabled persons. The ''Elephant Man'' was a horribly physically disabled person, but he possessed a great degree of intelligence. Although mistreated as a person, ideally, he still had the rights which other persons possessed.
2. Should a creature such as Harry be kept safe so science can study him? Obviously, we need to define what is meant by ''study.'' Second, we need to define (assuming experiments and studies would be allowed) what kinds of studies could be done. Would Harry have the same rights as a human involved in experiments? Would Harry be treated as an animal?
3. Finally, and this would be an interesting topic for extensive research, should computers be granted rights? If we grant rights based on intelligence, would the computer have rights? Is there more than intelligence involved in the granting of rights? What if a computer were programmed to exhibit human characteristics? This may seem like rather silly points, but the possibility of androids, and how we, as a society, might relate to them, poses some rather interesting questions.

PHILOSOPHICAL PROBLEM SHEET #17

One Man's Meat
Is Another Man's Poison

PROBLEM:

Six friends were on a mountain climbing trip to Alaska. They were miles away from any settlement and had no communication with anyone other than themselves. The feeling of isolation was very appealing to all members of the group. Suddenly, an avalanche occurred on what was thought to be safe climbing ground. The avalanche instantly killed two of the party.

Diane, Jeremy, and Lynn were weakened and in a terrible situation. Their food had been lost in the avalanche. Due to the freezing cold, it was necessary for them to eat in order to have the energy for the hard hike ahead. If they were to get to the nearest outpost, they would need plenty to eat. No one would be looking for them for several days. Hiking out of the mountain was their only chance for survival. Since the group now had no food, they all glanced at each other and then the bodies of their dead friends.

"I know there is little chance of getting rescued within the next few days," said Diane. "I also know if we stay here we will either freeze or starve to death. However, I cannot allow the eating of human flesh, especially that of our best friends, to assure my survival. I am not a cannibal. My culture and my philosophy will not allow me to do this. For me, the question is, 'Shall we die like humans or like animals?' I, for one, choose to die like a human being. I made the choice to climb knowing the dangers. I accept death as a possible consequence. I cannot lower myself to eat human flesh."

"Diane, I admire what you are saying," Jeremy responded. "However, I, for one, do not choose to die if I can do anything at all to save my own life. I have too much to live for. I have a mother, father and several brothers and sisters. I love these people. I have plans for my life. I am horrified and greatly saddened by our friends' deaths. I am sure that they would want us to survive any way we could. They are dead. There is nothing we can do for them. However, their death can give us life. Without their flesh we will die when we could have lived. The desire for life precedes every other consideration at this time. Diane, we must have food to live!"

Lynn responded, "I hear what both of you are saying. Diane feels it is more proper to live and if necessary die with honor as she perceives it. Jeremy believes it is better to live than to die. Since our friends are dead, they can provide us life. I am uncertain as to what to do. I will let you two decide and will go along with your decision. You must both agree on the same course of action. You must think of each other's needs as well as your own. After you decide, let me know your decision. However, whatever is decided, the reasons behind the decision must be acceptable ones.''

ACTIVITY:
Suddenly and unexpectedly, your three friends turn to you. Diane, Jeremy, and Lynn agree that it is you who must decide. They will follow your wishes. It is either life or death. Perhaps it means being human or being an animal. Remembering the concern for good reasons and intentions, you decide the best thing for your group to do is. . .

QUESTIONS:
1. According to the story, how would Diane describe a human being?
2. What is it that makes us human?
3. For the survivors in the story, what makes one human?
4. For whom in the story is the eating of human flesh a moral consideration?
5. Is morality determined by human beings or by the situations in which humans find themselves?
6. In the U.S., cannibalism is looked upon with disgust. In other parts of the world, cannibalism is accepted. Is cannibalism a social or a moral issue?
7. What is the connection between morality and social values?
8. In what ways might morality be determined by a culture?
9. What are some examples of taught morality?
10. Are these examples based on reason, emotion, or other considerations?

EXTENSION:
This is one of the most popular of the Philosophical Problem Sheets. It contains an interesting philosophical problem: the dilemma of physiological need of staying alive in relation to the ''spiritual'' need of maintaining human dignity. One could argue that this distinction is one based on social norms. We live in a society in which cannabilism is considered barbaric and evil. However, our society does not have to resort to cannabilism to

stay alive. In individual cases, cannabilism has been used to stay alive. The argument could have been that staying alive—even through the eating of human flesh—is more moral than allowing all members of a party to die from starvation. Obviously, this is against the "normal" ideas of society but extraordinary situations demand extraordinary actions.

There is also the issue of eating friends rather than companions or strangers. Would a friend who was killed in an accident want to be eaten in order for another to stay alive? Would this individual feel that the maintaining of dignity based on societal and perhaps ethical norms was more important than the survival of an individual or group of individuals? Depending on the situation and the possibility of rescue, the issue could be death with or without honor.

Obviously, there are other considerations. The authors would be interested in hearing from you about how you decided to use the activity and the reaction of the students! You can write to the authors in care of Trillium Press.

Cutting Off The Juice

PROBLEM:
Your best friend is gravely ill and is suffering greatly. The doctors have told him, his family and some of his friends there is no chance of recovery. The doctors are unsure exactly when your friend will die. Death could come anytime within the next three weeks. Your friend is being kept alive by a machine. This machine helps facilitate the functioning of the heart and lungs. However the pain of your friend is getting more and more severe. The hospital simply cannot administer any drugs which are strong enough to alleviate his pain. Your friend has stated over and over that he would rather die than continue to suffer such pain. Obviously, unplugging the machine could help facilitate his death. However, due to being immobilized, he is unable to reach the machine and "pull the plug." The doctors, although sympathetic with the plight of the patient, do not have the authority to remove the machine. This authority would take a court order and could involve months of hearings. Clearly this patient will not last that long. In addition, you have heard some doctors argue that the job of a hospital is to prolong life, not take it.

ACTIVITY:
Your friend begins to beg you to pull the plug on the machine and help him die. This is the only apparent way to relieve his suffering. In the eyes of the law, you realize that pulling the plug could constitute a criminal indictment, possibly murder. Yet it is hard to see your friend suffer such great pain. You have decided that there are four possible alternatives:

1.   You could tell your friend you will go through the courts. Perhaps with an emotional appeal, a court would agree to quickly hear your plea to allow this individual to "die as he wished." However you realize this is a longshot. Even if a court does decide for your friend, someone may appeal the decision. Therefore this alternative offers little chance of success.

2.   You could pull the plug on the machine. Hopefully no one would come into the room until after your friend's death. His suffering would be over and his wish granted. You realize that there is a possibility that

you could be charged with murder. Your defense, in court, would be to argue that you were fulfilling the request of your best friend; that you were helping him die with dignity instead of remaining in great pain.

3.   You could walk away and do nothing. Your friend will die and his suffering will be over. If you pull the plug, you could face a criminal conviction and a prison sentence. This could ruin your future.

4.   You could pay someone to figure out a way to facilitate the death of your friend. This person could then act out this plan. This would free you from actually killing your friend but you would have "helped" your friend if this plan were to succeed.

With time passing rapidly and your friend suffering more and more pain, the time to act is now. For these reasons, you decide that the best course of action is to. . .

QUESTIONS:

1.   According to the above scenario, how is your best friend being kept alive?

2.   What is his present condition?

3.   Should an individual be allowed to choose when s/he will die? Should it matter whether this person is in extreme pain?

4.   Should an individual or hospital be allowed to "pull the plug" on a patient and let this person die?

5.   What should be the criteria to allow such a decision?

6.   Suppose you were to form a panel to help decide the criteria to allow euthanasia. Who should make up this panel?

7.   In America, people believe they have the right to "pursue happiness." In what way could permitting the plug to be pulled be considered a "pursuit of happiness?"

8.   Could death be considered happy? Pleasant?

EXTENSIONS:

Obviously the above scenario is an example of an appeal for euthanasia. This issue is beginning to come to the forefront of our society and our consciousness. There are additional considerations which can add much to the discussion and philosophical issues involving the euthanasia question. Following are concepts which can be used to further the discussion:

Active vs. Passive Euthanasia

Let us assume that euthanasia can be allowed under certain conditions. As an example, a person several years ago, authored a living will. In this will it was stated that nothing was to be done which would sustain life unless this person would have a reasonable chance of recovery. This person now has a disease from which there is no chance of recovery. In addition this person is in extreme pain. The hospital agrees not to provide any artificial means to prolong the life.

The family does not want to see their loved one suffer. They ask if it is possible for the hospital to give something which would end the suffering of their loved one. This is the difference between active and passive euthanasia. It is possible to argue that it would be more moral to provide active euthanasia than passive euthanasia? After all, should persons with no chance of recovery be required to live in pain?

Obviously there are considerations which come into play. What should be the criteria that would establish the use of active euthanasia? Should the suffering person be the only one who could give permission? Would it be possible to argue that anyone who would wish to die is irrational? Should only hospitals or doctors be allowed to carry out euthanasia?

In addition, there is another consideration which must be taken into account. This involves the so-called "wedge" argument. Roughly speaking, the argument goes as follows: Say I allow a person to select active euthanasia. This person has been suffering greatly and clearly desires to end this life. I, being a doctor, after conferring with his friends (in some cases, it could be close friends or people who know and care for this person), administer a lethal injection which causes death. Another person comes along and desires the same treatment. This person is in pain, but does not appear to be as severe as the first person. The argument could then be made that whenever I start allowing active euthanasia, a "wedge" forms which will slowly expand the circumstances in which I will allow euthanasia. Indeed this wedge argument can be used in various other circumstances including abortion.

PHILOSOPHICAL ESSAY
Glaucon's Challenge

Background

In 1951, Edgar S. Brightman reminded us that a values conflict was raging in the world. Being called into question are freedom, reason, the rights of man, the worship of God, and the love of truth, beauty, and goodness. In recent times nothing has represented this conflict more strongly than the space shuttle tragedy of January, 1986. In the grief, confusion, and anger which followed that tragic explosion, the shuttle program lost its innocence. After a four-month investigation, a presidential commission concluded that the catastrophe was "an accident rooted in history," that is, NASA's acceptance of growing risks in trying to cut costs and meet an increasingly ambitious schedule.

As astronaut Capt. Frederick Hauck said, "Although the technical problems were coming faster than the solutions, the launch dates remained firm. Then, Challenger exploded."

Hauck went on to say, "Morals were not involved in the Challenger accident. I don't think anyone willingly subverted the system within NASA." The question of moral responsibility is an important question, one we perhaps wish would go away. In today's world of military buildup, totalitarianism, materialistic practices, and ruthless competition, it is not a question which we can easily ignore.

In the decades since Brightman made his observations about our world, a new and sustained interest in ethics and moral inquiry has surfaced and not only among members of the philosophical community, but among other professional groups as well. In science, medicine, politics, business, industry, education, and religion, ethical issues and ethical decision-making is now an important concern.

Because ethical inquiry and the problems associated with the proper application of ethical norms have become such an important focus in today's world of complex interrelationships, both business and political, a reassessment of many of the key issues relative to ethical decision-making and ethical justification needs to be undertaken by us.

As evidence of this concern over ethical norms, we can point to several popular books of recent vintage which voice a singular theme in calling for the moral evaluation of life and the conditions of living our lives in more humane ways. Toffler's *The Third Wave*, Capra's *The Turning Point*, and Sperry's *Science and Moral Priority* represent books which lie outside the domain of professional philosophy, but which call for a reassessment of moral norms and the development of a new moral paradigm—a paradigm broad enough to encompass both individual behaviors and the ecological care of the environment as well. Accordingly, the moral principles called for by these men will be holistic and specie neutral as their purpose is directed at both the human community and the relationship between human modes of living and the environmental demands of the planet itself.

Why Be Moral?
Needless to say, for young and old alike, the age in which we live today is a time in which new ideas and new ways of living that will eventually shape the history of intellectual thought and practical behavior must struggle for recognition and, some sort of application. The history of moral philosophy can be understood as a continuing dialogue about these ideas and ways; a dialogue that gathers its momentum from creative argumentation that intersects the many varied points of view that philosophers often take. The philosopher, like the child, cannot help but poke and pull at these ideas, looking for fresh territory for intellectual tilling and eventual harvesting.

During the past decades, such has characterized the history of the debate about a correct answer to the question, ''Why be moral?''; a question which, for many, still remains unclear, controversial, and inscrutable. One could safely say that in the history of moral philosophy, no other question has served as the nucleus of a meta-moral debate which has as long and pervasive a life-span. The issues of moral definition and moral justification have been a most persistent ''thorn in the flesh'' for any person seeking to conceptualize and establish a workable morality as either a goal to obtain or a pattern for everyday living.

In the *Republic*, we find Socrates and his philosophical adversaries, the Sophists, struggling with this question. At this moment in history, the question, ''Why be moral?'' is phrased as ''Why should men be morally virtuous?'' It is suggested that the weaker members of society value justice because justice, as the force of the law, restrains even the stronger from misusing his strength. It is reasoned by some that, if a person were certain that his own actions would go undetected and that, if one could not possibly be caught and punished, then that person—and all like him—would take advantage of his fellow man. It is further suggested by them that injustice is more profitable than justice, provided a person is able to escape detection.

In the story of Gyges' Ring (a magical ring the wearing of which renders a person invisible), Glaucon says:

Suppose now that there were two such magic rings, and the just put on one of them and the unjust the other; no man can be imagined to be of such iron nature that he would stand fast in justice. No man would keep his hands off what was not his own when he could safely take what he liked out of the market, or go into houses and lie with anyone at his pleasure, or kill or release from prison whom he would, and in all respects be like a God among men. Then the actions of the just would be as the actions of the unjust; they would both come at last to the same point. And this we may truly affirm to be a great proof that a man is just, not willingly or because he thinks that justice is any good to him individually, but of necessity, for wherever any one thinks that he can safely be unjust, there he is unjust. For all men believe in their hearts that injustice is far more profitable to the individual than justice, and he who argues as I have been supposing, will say that they are right.

Plato, *Republic*, II, 359ff

As a teacher of gifted students, you will hear students ask the same questions being asked here: "But, why do I have to do so and so, or be so and so, when no one else is or when it doesn't make any difference to anyone else anyway?" Just as in recent times moral philosophers have renewed their interest in the question, "Why be moral?", your students too will be interested in this question. But don't jump too quickly to answer it. First, following the procedures outlined in this chapter, allow time for an adequate analysis of the concept of morality and the moral point of view. It is imperative that the concept be clearly stated by students and that its conceptualization be fully understood by them before moving on to other matters.

Secondly, after students have worked on the proper conceptualization of the moral point of view, the time will come when reasons must be given for following the rules of morality over the dictates of selfish-interest or egoism. The justification of morality is an important undertaking. Here students will reformulate ideas and beliefs and begin the process of understanding the role of reason in everyday life. Make sure students understand the difference between a reason and a cause—that is, between a justification and an explanation of behavior. Have them give examples to help explain and justify their points of view. These procedures will help students as they later use these "considered" moral judgments in moral decision-making and problem-solving.

We end as we began. An ideological conflict is now going on in our world. Are our students prepared to enter into these debates, tackle these issues, formulate intelligent and reasoned opinions, and make enlightened moral decisions? The conflict is not merely political, nor is it primarily social or intellectual. Rather, it is a struggle in the minds of men and women, boys and girls, about ultimate values — the nature of the values which they hold and wish to defend. It is time to begin.

CONCEPTUAL SCHEME FOUR: KNOWLEDGE AND UNDERSTANDING

GOALS AND OBJECTIVES

SCHEMATIC GOAL:

Students will identify the nature, sources, scope, and limits of human knowledge.

This study takes as its major interest knowledge and understanding. It will focus its attention upon the nature, sources, scope, and limits of human knowledge. This study begins quite broadly with an analysis of the "kinds of knowing" open to the human species and then gradually narrows its vision in order to raise the issues and draw the distinctions associated with the problem of the criteria for knowledge. This major philosophical problem will be analyzed in the following paragraphs and then be dealt with in the section on philosophical problems.

KINDS OF KNOWING...

There are many different kinds of knowing. More exactly, there are many different uses of the word "know." Unless one is extremely careful, any single use of "know" may be ambiguous. Our purpose is to call attention to some of these uses and then focus on one or two that are philosophically germane to the purposes of this chapter.

When a person says, "I know Sam Smith," at least four different meanings are being intended:

1.   familiarity,

2.   recognition,
3.   anticipatory abilities, or
4.   empathy.

One knows other people as a function of the extent and intensity of empathic contact one has with them. But to say that one knows a person who died before one was born ("I know Descartes") seems a little odd. One may know one's son or daughter out of shared experiences of personal contact. This knowledge may also come from a complete set of physical and affective sensations in which one's daughter or son is the focus of attention. But, at this time in history, one cannot KNOW Descartes in these ways. One's present knowledge of the great French mathematician comes from inference and someone else's authority.

The word "know" has other uses as well. For example, if one of my students tells me, "I know the multiplication tables through ten," then this student is really saying that she or he has the ABILITY to recite these tables on demand. But having acquired a certain skill through drill and reinforcement is not the same as knowing a close friend or an ancient figure in history.

When a person talks about knowing a close friend, is s/he talking more about his/her skills as a knower, or about the rapport which exists between themselves and their friend?

KNOWLEDGE-HOW AND KNOWLEDGE-THAT. . .

The knowledge displayed in reciting, riding a bike, threading a needle, or putting on one's shoes is called "knowledge-how." Some individuals have said that just about all knowledge comes down to one or another form of knowledge-how.

But does knowledge-how cover the kind of knowledge affirmed in such statements as, "I know that Alan Sheppard was the first American in space" or "I know that today is Tuesday?" When the claim to know is made in statements such as these, one appears to be referring to something that is true, or asserting that something has, in fact, happened, or that this particular bit of information is true. This kind of knowledge is called "knowledge-that."

To make the distinction between knowledge-how and knowledge-that even more clear, consider the following examples:

1.   A mentally handicapped student is one of the fastest on the swim team. This student is a very slow learner and reads on a level far below her

or his age. Thus, this student has never read anything about swimming techniques, i.e., what goes on when a person swims and why. Although this student cannot read very well, he can swim like a fish. One can say that this student "knows how" to swim quite well.

2.   On the other hand, a certain teacher is quite knowledgeable about swimming and swimming techniques. This teacher has read the best books on the subject of swimming, observed many swimmers, and has written articles about swimming techniques for sports magazines. Yet, there is one thing this teacher cannot do—swim. The teacher knows a great many facts about swimming, but, once in the water, sinks like a rock. One can say that this teacher "knows that" certain techniques are preferable for better swimming, but one cannot say that this teacher "knows how" to swim.

Thus, the basic difference between "knowledge-how" and "knowledge-that" is the difference between understanding and doing. It is what many rural people for years have called the difference between "horse-sense" and "book learning." Our mentally handicapped student knows HOW to swim, but does not know—technically and factually—very much about swimming. This student has the physique, motor skills, and practice it takes to become a great swimmer. On the other hand, our teacher has all the knowledge a person needs to understand swimming, but cannot perform the act itself.

To further understand this distinction, consider another difference between knowledge-how and knowledge-that. Knowledge-how can be blocked by interfering with a person's motor equipment, without ever attacking the person's thought processes. Suppose the good swimmer breaks a leg; this would interfere with her or his swimming performance. The damage could even be permanent. Knowledge-that cannot be blocked so easily. Knowledge-that is COGNITION or understanding and can be disturbed only when the brain itself is disturbed. Of course, one could reduce the human species to only gross motor skills and say that all cognitions are simply complex and subtle motor skills. But this would not destroy the distinction between knowledge-how and knowledge-that.

NECESSARY CONDITIONS OF KNOWLEDGE-THAT. . .

When an individual makes a successful claim to know something FOR SURE, what is involved? What is it that that person claims and what does it take to make the claim work? The answer to these questions involves the clarification of the necessary conditions that any claim to knowledge-that must meet. There are THREE necessary conditions for knowledge-that:

1.   ASSERTIVE CONTENT: In the first place, one must make a distinction between COGNITIVE and COGNITION. Cognitive is an adjective which says that something CAN constitute knowledge-that. Cognition is a noun which tells us that certain items in a person's experience DO constitute knowledge-that. Here are several examples:
     a.   "I will get a raise next year."
     b.   "There is life on Mars."
     c.   "August 14, 1979 is a Tuesday."
     d.   "The left burner on my stove is still on."
     Statements (a) and (b) are cognitive claims. They tell one that if certain conditions are realized—"that I actually get a raise next year," or "that someday some being finds life on the planet Mars"—then they CAN BECOME cognitions. These two hypothetical statements are expressions of possible (contingent) states. This is one reason why they are stated in the conditional (if, then) modality.
     Examples (c) and (d) are not only cognitive, they also express cognitions. They are actually true. All that it takes for a claim to be cognitive is the possibility of its being true. This is what is meant by "assertive content." All of the above examples are cognitive; they all possess assertive content. Only examples (c) and (d) are actually true assertions.
     Let's look at the first two examples again. It has already been said that these two statements are cognitive. They genuinely affirm the possibility of something being the case. But when these statements are subjected to testing, one may find that what they assert is NOT actually true at all. Thus, they may remain as unrealized possibilities. One may not get a raise next year or scientists may someday discover that there is no life on Mars. Thus, these claims are false. But, they are still cognitive. They merely fail to express a cognition. Any straight-forward assertion that one normally can understand is a cognitive assertion, but it is not necessarily a cognition.

The first necessary condition for a claim to be counted as KNOWL-
EDGE is that it be cognitive. Knowledge begins with having some
genuine cognitive content.

2.   TRUTH: All that is required for a statement to be believed at some
      time or another is that it have some cognitive content. The content
      need not be obviously or even probably true for people to believe it.
      It makes perfectly good sense to talk about "false beliefs." Most
      beliefs have some cognitive content; they normally assert that something
      is the case or that something has happened in the past. If it is later
      discovered that the assertions are false, then it can be said that the
      person has a false belief.
         On the other hand, it makes no sense at all to talk about "false
      knowledge." This is the place where belief and knowledge part com-
      pany. Thus, a second necessary condition is that what is known must,
      in fact, be true.
         Believing an assertion is not, in itself, enough to purchase knowl-
      edge. A belief may be mistaken. One's beliefs OUGHT to be respon-
      sible to the truth. If they are not, then they are not knowledge.

3.   EVIDENCE: A cognition must have both cognitive content and truth,
      but these alone are not enough. Even though a person might make a
      true claim, one would still have the right to say that the person did
      not really know for sure. The statement in question may have been a
      lucky guess or a coincidence. The reason one is not willing to say that
      the person KNEW FOR SURE is because the person did not incorporate
      some kind of EVIDENCE-CONNECTION into what was said.
         Knowledge demands more than the logical possibility of evidence;
      it demands some amount of actual available evidence. It is necessary
      that there be some objective and stable criteria against which different
      kinds of evidence can be measured. Such evidence will be used to
      weigh one's knowledge claims. The criteria for evidence will be judged
      by its pragmatic value (its usefulness and effectiveness in settling
      disputes and making judgments in the workaday world).

      a.   CRITERIA FOR EVIDENCE
            i.   RELEVANCE — It must have something to do with what
                  is at stake.
            ii.   NONCIRCULARITY — It must not simply restate the claim
                  itself.

iii. INTELLIGIBILITY — It must be comprehensible.

iv. NONAMBIGUITY — The evidence must be straight-forward, clear and unequivocal.

v. CONSISTENCY — The evidence must not contradict itself.

vi. PUBLIC — Effective evidence must be open to public confirmation.

vii. FREEDOM — The evidence must be free of bias, conflict of interest, etc.

viii. VIABILITY — Effective evidence must be formulated in terms of a viable theory or hypothesis.

(Hall, James. *Knowledge, Belief and Transcendence*. Boston: Houghton Mifflin Co., 1974.)

b. KINDS OF EVIDENCE

The following diagram, adapted from Joseph Royce's *The Encapsulated Man,* explains the four basic kinds of evidence or sources of knowledge—thinking, feeling, sensing, and believing. These four sources of knowledge reveal a pattern of approaches to reality and consequent understandings. They must be evaluated by the criteria of evidence listed above. The following page outlines a summary of the evidence connections for knowledge-that.

AFFECTIVE PROCESS	APPROACHES TO REALITY	UNDERSTANDINGS OF REALITY
Thinking	Rationalism	Logical/Illogical
Feeling	Intuitionism	Insight/No Insight
Sensing	Empiricism	Perception/Misprision
Believing	Authoritarianism	Ideology/Delusion
EVIDENCE	**SYSTEM**	**RESULT**

THE SOURCES OF KNOWLEDGE
FIGURE 7

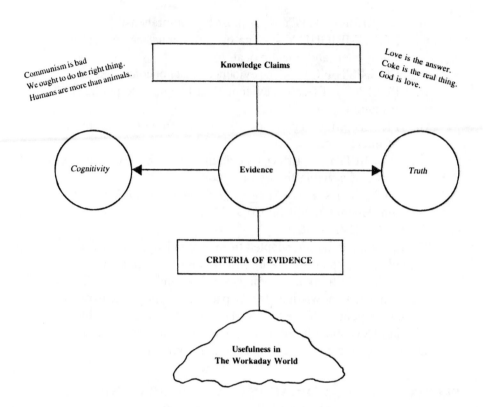

EVIDENCE CONNECTIONS FOR KNOWLEDGE-THAT
FIGURE 8

SUGGESTED CURRICULUM OUTLINE. . .

Below is a suggested curriculum outline for teaching the conceptual scheme, knowledges and understanding. The ideas, goals, and topics will assist both teacher and student in studying the major themes presented in this chapter.

I.   UNIT ONE: The Sources of Knowledge
     UNIT OBJECTIVE:
          Students will identify the sources of knowledge within the affective process of being human.
     TASK DESCRIPTIONS:
     A.   KNOWLEDGES
          Students will. . .
          1.   Identify the four affective processes which are the sources of human knowledge.
          2.   Outline the character of each affective process which is a source of human knowledge.
          3.   State the implications of each affective process which is a source of human knowledge.
          4.   Give examples of each affective process which is a source of human knowledge.
          5.   Point out the differences between ''knowledge-how'' and ''knowledge-that.''
          6.   Give examples of ''knowledge-how'' and ''knowledge-that.''
     B.   CONCEPTS
          Students will define the following terms:
          1.   Thinking
          2.   Feeling
          3.   Sensing
          4.   Believing
          5.   Rationalism
          6.   Empiricism
          7.   Intuitionism
          8.   Authoritarianism
          9.   Knowledge-how
          10. Knowledge-that
     C.   VALUES
          Students will. . .
          1.   State personal intuitions and beliefs clearly and unambiguously.

     2.   Arrange their sources of knowing in a knowledge hierarchy.
     3.   Demonstrate commitment to objective reasoning.
     4.   Use the objective approach in problem solving.
     5.   Identify their own knowledge strengths and weaknesses.

D.   SKILLS

Students will. . .

1. Evaluate the role of each affective process in their search for knowledge and truth.
2. Give examples of both ideologies and beliefs.
3. Compare the different characteristics of knowledge and opinion.
4. Identify knowledge statements supported only by reason.
5. Identify knowledge statements supported only by sensation.
6. Compare what is known by reason with what is known by sensation.
7. Ask questions of speakers or class members, all of which require them to cite the sources of their knowledge and justify their approach to knowledge.
8. Analyze the statement, "I know that it is snowing in Claremont, North Carolina" by diagramming the path to support its truth or falsity.

II.   UNIT TWO: Developing A Criteria for Knowing

UNIT OBJECTIVE:

Students will select and justify (give reasons for) a method of knowing that is functional in the everyday world.

TASK DESCRIPTIONS:

A.   KNOWLEDGES

Students will. . .

1. Distinguish between cognition and cognitive.
2. Give examples of "false beliefs" that have been purported to be true throughout human history at one time or another.
3. Restate, in their own words, the standards by which different kinds of evidence can be measured.
4. Identify the "evidence connections" for the statement, "Humans are more than animals."
5. Illustrate the different kinds of evidence to which people appeal when they make a claim to know.

B.   CONCEPTS

Students will define the following terms:

1. Cognitive
2. Cognition
3. Truth
4. Evidence
5. Inductive Reasoning
6. Deductive Reasoning
7. Necessity
8. Contingency

C. VALUES

Students will. . .

1. Demonstrate a willingness to establish a criteria for knowing.
2. Demonstrate a willingness to assess personal beliefs by this criteria.
3. Modify those items, which they claim to know, by this criteria.
4. Identify which source of knowledge has dominated their life.
5. Integrate this criteria of knowing into their life.

D. SKILLS

Students will. . .

1. State a criteria of knowing and support it with strong reasoning.
2. Compare the characteristics of statements based on belief with those based on reason and/or sensation.
3. Evaluate basic beliefs by this criteria.
4. Assess their values for consistency and relevancy.
5. List the basic characteristics of contingent statements.
6. List the basic characteristics of necessarily true statements.
7. Answer the question, ''Are statements of contingency and necessity both statements of facts?''
8. Apply previously learned ideas about knowledge in order to decide how one would know the truth or falsity of the following:
    (a) That a bottle of medicine costs $5.
    (b) That ice cream is good.
    (c) The color of a basketball.
    (d) That God exists.
    (e) That your friend has a pain in his elbow.
    (f) That it is or is not raining outside.
    (g) That brotherhood is a good and positive value.

III. UNIT THREE: Inquiry Skills
UNIT OBJECTIVE:
Students will apply higher level thinking abilities to important human problems and to everyday learning experiences.
TASK DESCRIPTIONS:
A. KNOWLEDGES
Students will. . .
1. Describe the unique characteristics of a person, place, thing, event, process, or idea (observing).
2. Identify cause-and-effect relationships (explaining, synthesizing).
3. Apply known cause-and-effect relationships to possible future events in order to generate probable consequences of existing ideas (predicting, evaluating).
4. Contrast existing alternatives in order to make value judgments for future action (choosing, analyzing, evaluating).
5. Use the scientific method of knowing (apply your criteria of knowing).
B. CONCEPTS
Students will define the following terms:
1. Observing
2. Explaining
3. Predicting
4. Choosing
5. Concept
6. Generalization
7. Scientific Method
C. VALUES
Students will. . .
1. Demonstrate an understanding of the strengths and weaknesses of their thought processes.
2. Demonstrate a willingness to develop their thinking abilities to more efficient levels.
3. Formulate a continuum of thinking skills for future development.
4. Demonstrate industry, punctuality, and self-discipline.
5. Display appropriate thinking skills in and outside of class.
6. Formulate a life plan which harmonizes abilities, interests, and ideas about the future.

PHILOSOPHICAL PROBLEM

The Problem Of Claiming To Know

The problem of knowledge can be stated in the form of the question: "What can I say that I know for sure?" That is, when is a person JUSTIFIED in making a claim to know something? Philosophically, this question seeks a logical right to make a claim to knowledge.

In order to answer this question, the student has to examine various kinds of statements, each of which makes a claim to knowledge. The purpose of such an examination is to see what one can logically accept as GOOD REASONS for saying that each of these statements is true or false.

Fundamentally, the problem of knowledge reveals itself in a series of questions:

1. What is the distinction between knowledge and true opinion?
2. How does one decide, in any particular case, whether she or he knows something; that is, what are the criteria of knowing?
3. What counts as adequate EVIDENCE for one's knowledge of things? What is the stopping place for giving such evidence?
4. How does one know things that are not directly evident, those things that may be deduced from other things, but are themselves unobserved?
5. How does one know that the truths of reason (logic and mathematics) are reliable?
6. Finally, how does one know that certain metaphysical "things" in fact exist—such as God—or the existence of physical objects beyond a person's sensory experiences?

TYPES OF FACTS:
What would be some good reasons for saying that the following two statements are true?
1. "Rain is falling in Claremont."
2. "Every cube has twelve edges of equal length."

NOTE: The teacher should discuss each of these statements separately with the students. Permit each student to share with the class why s/he thinks that they MIGHT or MUST be true. Also, ask the class HOW one in fact knows that they are true or false. What the teacher needs to emphasize is the method of knowing rather than what is known.

1. *"Rain is falling in Claremont."* Statements of this type, (A is B) where the intention of the statement is to express a state of affairs holding within the observable world, have the following characteristics:

   a. CONTINGENCY: The truth of the statement is dependent upon certain conditions being present in the publicly observable world.

   b. A POSTERIORI: The method of discovering whether rain is actually falling in Claremont at a certain time is inductive. The inductive method is dependent, in the final analysis, upon sensory experience. One should go to Claremont and SEE if it is or is not raining.

   c. SYNTHETIC: The truth of the statement, "Rain is falling in Claremont," depends on a synthesis of union (correspondence) holding between the subject "rain" and the predicate "is falling in Claremont." A synthetic statement which is both contingent and a posteriori can be denied without contradiction. Thus, it makes sense to say, if, in fact, one goes to Claremont and does not observe any rain falling, "It is not raining in Claremont at this time." No contradiction is involved.

2. *"Every cube has twelve edges of equal length."* Statements of this type (A is B), where the intention of the statement is to give a definition, have the following features:

   a. NECESSITY: When presented correctly, according to the funda-mental rules of mathematics, this statement is always true, regard-less of whether a cube actually exists in the observable world. It is a truth of reason, not observation.

   b. A PRIORI: The method of discovering the truth of this statement is mental reasoning, not physical experience. The statement, "Every cube has twelve edges of equal length," is true by the meaning of its words. If someone were to ask for the meaning of the word "cube," the correct response must include the pro-vision of "twelve edges of equal length."

   c. ANALYTIC: The truth of this statement is found by deducing the predicate "has twelve edges of equal length" from the subject "every cube." A fundamental feature of analytic statements is that to DENY the truth of the predicate leads to self-contradiction. The subject and the predicate mean the same thing. To deny this is contradictory. (See: Westphal, *Activity*, for an excellent discus-sion of these concepts.)

Once the teacher has made these distinctions with the class, the students should be encouraged to produce statements of both types and compare them with these distinctions for "family resemblances." This exercise is fundamental to studies in the theory of knowledge, for one is making a distinction between:

truths of reason (logic and mathematics)
and
truths of observation (the inductive method).

For practice, try these borderline cases:
1.   All blackbirds are black.
2.   All black birds are black.
3.   I exist.
4.   The President of the United States exists.
5.   There is a sharp pain in my elbow.
6.   There are correct moral rules which everyone ought to obey.

CONCLUSION:

Today, most philosophers agree that our knowledge of the FACTUAL WORLD is derived from sensory experience or sense perception. Fundamentally, this is the Empiricist's approach to knowledge although an element of Rationalism is added to it. The Rationalists seek knowledge of the "unquestionable." That is, knowledge upon which one can rely completely.

The nearest we have come to this kind of knowledge is through mathematics. Through mathematical methods (utilizing computer technology) scientists have been able to organize the data of sensory experience in such ways as to give us the dimension of predictability. This joining of induction and deduction is generally called the scientific method.

Although the dimension of mathematics has been able to shore up inductive reasoning, individuals have generally questioned the inductive method because it gives us only statistical probability and not the absolute certainty that many individuals seek. In the following paragraphs an argument will be presented in favor of the inductive method. Go over this argument very carefully with its reasoning. A list of difficulties with the argument will follow at the end of this section.

PHILOSOPHICAL PROBLEM

The Problem Of Induction

THE NATURE OF INDUCTION

Consider the following statement (prediction): "It is going to snow very soon." Based upon one's observations of a number of occasions in the past which accurately resemble the circumstances which now prevail, one can say with SOME CERTAINTY that it is going to snow very soon.

An INDUCTIVE GENERALIZATION is the following type:

"Whenever conditions X1, X2, and X3 are present, one may rightly expect the result Y."

The concept of induction has been defended by Bertrand Russell and David Hume. Russell includes the concept of "probability" in his defense. Russell concludes that when an item of one's experience of a certain sort A has been discovered to be ASSOCIATED WITH another item of one's experience of a certain sort B, the more cases in which A and B have been associated, the greater the PROBABILITY that they will be associated in a fresh case in which one of them is known to be present.

For example, in North Carolina snowfall is usually produced in winter by a low front moving across the Gulf states in association with a polar air mass (high) pushing down from Canada. When these two air masses meet, the result is usually snowfall. Even as I type this page, a polar air mass is pushing down from the north, and a low, organized two days ago in the Gulf of Mexico, is headed toward North Carolina. As a result of these conditions together with what has occurred in the past, the prediction for tonight and tomorrow is snow.

In the *Enquiry*, Hume felt that instances in the future of which one has had no experience must resemble those of which one has had experience. Hume's reasoning was that "the course of nature continues always uniformly the same."

The nature of inductive conclusions yields no absolute certainty. The principle of certainty needs to be qualified. With inductive predictions all one can conclude is that "the course of nature MOST LIKELY (it is highly probable) continues uniformly the same."

After thoroughly studying this problem with your students, permit them to write or discuss their criticism of it. They may wish to formulate a set of questions to ask Russell or Hume, in which case, you can let Russell and Hume answer them.

DIFFICULTIES WITH THIS ARGUMENT

1.   The principle of induction cannot be justified. All that a person has a right to claim is that "the course of nature HAS always continued to be the same." One cannot support the claim that nature WILL always continue to be the same. The future course of events might be radically different from the past regardless of how uniform they might have appeared before.
2.   The principle of induction is founded upon a principle that must be taken on FAITH alone. Scientifically, faith is not counted as solid evidence.
3.   Terms such as "associated with," "most likely," and "it is highly probable that" are void of any scientific meaning and precision. These terms must be explained and their use justified before the principle of induction can work.

SPECIAL NOTE. . .

The philosophical problems mentioned in this chapter on the theory of knowledge and those mentioned in Chapters Five, Six, and Seven are merely samples. They only scratch the surface of the marvelous world of philosophical inquiry that awaits you and your students.

But before diving in too heavily, it is advisable to choose one or two books mentioned in the Bibliography at the end of this book and study them carefully. If you really desire to teach this type of material, go back to school and take several Philosophy courses. They will be beneficial.

Boom, Boom. . . Out Go the Lights

PROBLEM:

A few years ago during a heavy thunder and lightning storm a munitions plant exploded. Lightning had been striking all around the plant. There was a tremendous blast of lightning. Immediately afterwards the plant exploded. Due to the severity of the explosion, special investigators were called to the site. They were hoping to learn why the explosion occurred. The knowledge obtained would help eradicate the possibility of an explosion like this occurring again. The three investigators developed three hypotheses about the origin of the explosion. They reflected three views of the relationship between the explosion of the munitions plant and the lightning:

(1)   coincidence,

(2)   cause-and-effect, and

(3)   co-relational.

Will Blistor stated that the explosion occurred by COINCIDENCE. Lightning hit somewhere and shortly or immediately afterwards, the plant exploded. The lightning strike and the plant's explosion were two separate events which occurred nearly simultaneously.

Jill Cortex concluded that the explosion occurred by CAUSE-AND-EFFECT. Jill decided lightning was the cause of the plant's explosion. The cause had to precede the effect.

Laurie Placen determined that the lightning and the plant's explosion was CO-RELATIONAL. The co-relation exists between lightning, which causes sparks, and a munitions plant which is highly explosive. There is a relationship between a spark (lightning) when it comes into contact with a combustible material (munitions): An explosion will occur. Thus there is a co-relation between combustibility and sparks—an explosion.

ACTIVITY:

The company's president is responsible for examining the report before the findings are released to the public. Ms. Infeld concluded that the interpretations of the investigators were not in agreement with one another. In order to obtain a better understanding of the reports, Ms. Infeld decided you should provide further interpretations and state implications of the report. You are to explain how the various interpretations of the explosion would affect each investigator's report. You are also to give two examples of the terms COINCIDENCE, CAUSE-AND-EFFECT, and CO-RELATIONAL, separate from the munitions plant explosion, in order to help clarify the meanings of the terms.

QUESTIONS:
1.   What were the three possible explanations of the explosion?
2.   How do the definitions of the terms resemble each other?
3.   How are the definitions of terms different?
4.   What evidence would be necessary to determine the cause-and-effect relationship of a particular incident?
5.   Define the terms induction and deduction.
6.   How would scientists use deduction and induction to help develop scientific theories?
7.   What are some of the risks of making predictions based on a scientific method?

EXTENSION:
The issue of cause and effect can be a most interesting topic of inquiry.

In our house, we have a television set which malfunctions. Whenever the pictures starts to roll, I quickly get up and slap the top. Generally, after one or two slaps, the picture stabilizes. However, about once an hour, I need to adjust the knobs.

I can assume that there is a cause-and-effect relationship. The cause, slapping the top of the set, results in the desired effect, a stable picture.

However, my wife is very patient. She will not get up and hit the set. Usually within a short period of time, the picture will stabilize on its own. She states that there is only a coincidence between my slap and the picture stabilizing.

How could we settle this difference of opinion?

There are many other instances when cause and effect can be confused with coincidence. Have the students brainstorm a list of incidents when cause and effect or coincidence could be used as an explanation of phenomena. How would one go about constructing a way to test and determine whether the incident was one or the other?

PHILOSOPHICAL PROBLEM SHEET #20
In My Opinion

PROBLEM:

Political debates have long been a popular means for voters to see and hear political hopefuls. Debates allow candidates to express their opinions and ideas on the issues. The prospective voters are able to hear the various views of the debaters. This allows voters to decide which candidate they would support in an election.

Recently, three political leaders, representing three political parties, debated on national television. They were Elvis Berdino from the New Wave Party, Ronald Stempe from the Old Hat Party, and Daphne O'Neil from the New Progressive Party. The candidates' positions varied from conservative to radical depending on the issue. On one important issue the debaters apparently maintained the same position. When asked if they favored the policy of massive defense spending the candidates answered as follows:

Elvis Berdino: "I FEEL we should continue our present level of defense military spending. We should increase the amount spent if necessary to keep up with inflation."

Ronald Stempe: "My OPINION is to continue and expand our present level of defense spending. Security is our most important concern."

Daphne O'Neil: "I BELIEVE only by continuing our present military spending can this country be secure. We must continue our present level of spending. We should also increase the spending if necessary."

The definition for feel, opinion, and belief are as follows:
1. feel—intuition/hunch
2. opinion—what a person thinks is true or false
3. belief—a strongly held opinion.

ACTIVITY:

Candidates often depend heavily on support from individuals to help finance their campaigns. You have decided to donate $1,000 to the candidate of your choice. The question of defense spending is the key consideration for the donation of the money. All the candidates appear very close on this issue. The difference is in the usage of the words feel, opinion, and believe (belief). Examine the above definitions of the words. Decide which word denotes the best stand on the issue. Then decide which candidate you would support. Give two reasons for your choice.

QUESTIONS:

1. How did the definition of the words feel, opinion, and belief differ?
2. The above defined words are similar and yet different. If you were expressing a view, how might you elaborate on your opinion to establish a more powerful statement?
3. What are ways individuals accumulate knowledge? Share knowledge?
4. What criteria should someone use in evaluating data?
5. In the use of logic one attempts to prove conclusions by the use of examples and reason. A logician tries to avoid the use of fallacies. One fallacy is called an appeal to authority. An example of this fallacy would be as follows: Jeremy stated, "I know this is true because my teacher said so." Jeremy is not giving reasons for the truthfulness of this statement. He states it is true only because his teacher said so. The teacher is his authority rather than reason. Thus, Jeremy committed a fallacy of appeal to authority. Can you think up other examples of an "appeal to authority" which is used as an explanation?

EXTENSION:

Let's look at "feeling," "opinion," and "belief" in a different manner. What is the difference between saying, "Tom has an educated opinion on this issue," and "Tom has an opinion on this issue?" Perhaps Tom is well educated and has a carefully considered opinion. However, by adding the word "educated," one might be more inclined to listen to Tom. The same might be said for feeling or belief. "Jerry has a strong feeling about this issue." "Linda has a firm belief about this issue."

Let us look at some other words which are used by individuals to lend authority to their comments. A person may say, "I have faith that man did not evolve from lower creatures." Another individual states, "I have empirical evidence which leads me to state that man evolved from more primitive creatures." Which opinion would you be more likely to accept as true? For some individuals, the word "faith" is very powerful. "I just have faith that I am right even if I cannot give any evidence." Others may put a limited value on the use of faith: "I prefer evidence rather than blind faith on this issue." Depending on the reader, key words might create opinions about an issue that another reader would find less convincing. A critical question is, "How do we determine what should be accepted as evidence when considering an issue?"

An interesting exercise would be to read regularly the paper or weekly news magazines. Note how individuals phrase key aspects of a story or idea. Another good exercise is to compare the reporting of the same story in several newspapers or news journals. Does the story always focus on the same material? How might certain key words be used to discuss the same idea? Is the same evidence used to support various positions?

PHILOSOPHICAL PROBLEM SHEET #21

Progress or Regress

PROBLEM:

The building firm of Pacer and Williams is planning to build a new shopping mall, on the outskirts of the city of Daniel. Daniel is a small city located in a mountainous region. The area is characterized by cool summers and heavy rainfall throughout the year. Opposed to the building of the mall is a group of environmental planners.

The proposed site is located on a flood plain. A flood plain is a flat area where a lot of water flows through from surrounding areas. The area of the proposed mall has been severely flooded twice within the last ten years. Since building a mall will disrupt the vegetation which helps control some of the water runoff, more water will be channeled into area creeks. The water will lack an area to flow properly and will "back up" and flood the area. This will not only affect the immediate area of the proposed mall but also the surrounding residential section.

The planners continue to state that besides the bad floods, this mountainous area has averaged one catastrophic flood every forty years. During the previous catastrophic floods, before it was developed, havoc was spread over the area. Developments (residential or commercial), if not properly planned, tend to create more run-off problems than most undeveloped lands. The effect of a major flood could be catastrophic to the surrounding area of the proposed building site.

The planners further argue that building the mall would spoil the aesthetic nature of the surrounding area. The field is presently used as a cow pasture. This pasture is located within one mile of the downtown area. This area creates a relaxing attitude for the nearby residents. Many residents have voiced their liking of the "little bit of country in the city."

The representatives of Pacer and Williams maintain the flood waters can be controlled. Engineers have learned much within the last few years on how to control water runoff. The mall would be constructed to insure the accumulated knowledge of the engineers would be used to the utmost of the builders' abilities. To answer the point made concerning a severe flood averaging once every forty years, they say that there is no reason to guarantee that this trend will continue in the future. The future is not "required" to follow the trends of the past. In conclusion, the representatives acknowledge that they are going to remove a cow pasture. However, the mall will be well designed with benches and trees. The design will attempt to fit into the mountain beauty rather than exist separately. The value of the cow pasture will be replaced with a different aesthetic.

ACTIVITY:

The issue divides many of the town's residents. The Town Council has heard both positions and will reach a decision within two days. The Council has developed eight criteria to help decide which side has better evidence in defending its position. The criteria are listed below.
1.   Relevance—it must have something to do with what is at stake.
2.   Noncircularity—it must not simply re-state the claim itself.
3.   Intelligibility—the claim must be comprehensible.
4.   Nonambiguity—the evidence must be straightforward, clear, and unequivocal.
5.   Consistency—the evidence must not contradict itself.
6.   Public—effective evidence must be open to public confirmation.
7.   Freedom—the evidence must be free of bias, conflict of interest, etc.
8.   Viability—evidence must be formulated in terms of a viable theory or hypothesis.

Divide the class into thirds, one group being the representatives of the builders; the second, the environmental planners; and the third, the council. Hold a full-scale hearing on the project, and then have the council decide on the basis of the eight criteria.

Alternatively, have each person act as a council member and give two reasons for deciding for one side or the other.

QUESTIONS:
1.   What are the reasons presented by the planners to stop construction of the mall?
2.   What reasons does Pacer and Williams give for building the mall?
3.   We take it for granted that the sun will rise every day. This is based on faith: The sun has always risen, it will continue to rise. In philosophy, this is called induction. Induction consists of studying the previous information and assigning a probability to a future outcome. What is an example of induction in the question of building the mall?

4.   What are other examples of induction?
5.   Can you imagine examples when the use of induction has failed to yield true predictions?
6.   Scientists often use induction within their scientific methods. Examine the "Criteria of Evidence." Next, develop additional criteria which would be useful for a scientist.
7.   Study the definition of "noncircularity." What are other examples of a circular argument?
8.   How would a scientist or philosopher attempt to be free of bias or conflict of interest in his/her claims?

EXTENSION:

The criteria in this example were used to help clarify the issue. We hope it also allowed the students to construct logical, cohesive arguments. Another critical tool to use in reasoning is to avoid the commitment of fallacies of argument. Howard Kahne in his book, *Logic and Philosophy,* defines a fallacy as:

> . . .an argument which should not persuade a rational person to accept its conclusion. And let's say that a person commits a fallacy, or reasons fallaciously, if he accepts the conclusion of a fallacious argument, and is guilty of a fallacy, or argues fallaciously, when he uses a fallacious argument in an attempt to covince someone of its conclusion.
>
> Of course, these definitions naturally lead one to ask which arguments should and which should not persuade a rational person. Roughly speaking, a person should not be persuaded by any argument which either (1) is invalid, or (2) has premises which should be doubted by that person or (3) although valid, suppresses pertinent evidence.

What follows is a method one might utilize in the teaching of fallacies of argument. Below are two fallacies, "appeal to force," and "appeal to authority." Have the students do the exercises. The book mentioned above will allow interested students to further expand their knowledge.

PHILOSOPHICAL PROBLEM

The Fallacy of Appeal To Authority

Sometimes a person may try to argue for a point by appealing to the feeling of respect or honor others may have toward some individual or source; however, the individual or source one uses is not an authority on the subject. When this type of argumentation is used, there is a fallacious appeal to authority. This fallacy is frequently committed in advertising when a famous actor does a commercial for a product that he or she is not in a special authoritative position to recommend. (However, one may legitimately appeal to an authority to back up a claim if the person is indeed an authority on the matter, in which case no fallacy has been committed since such an appeal does constitute evidence for the claim.)

EXAMPLE:
Sue and Max, both psychology majors, are taking a course in criminal justice. Today the professor explained some theories about the causes of criminal behavior and gave some evidence for each. After class they compared their ideas about which theory seemed to be more plausible. Sue had a difficult time making up her mind about which theory she was more inclined to accept since she thought that at least two of them made some good points. Though Max agreed, he said, "Personally, I can't accept any of those explanations." When Sue asked why, he replied. "Because my minister said in his sermon last Sunday that the reason people commit crimes is that they haven't been saved from sin."

EXERCISES:
1. Why is Max guilty of a fallacious appeal to authority?
2. Suppose Max's minister had an advanced degree in psychology, had worked extensively with criminals, and had cited evidence in his sermon to support a theory of criminal behavior. If Max wanted to quote his minister as evidence for accepting one of the theories, what types of points should he make in order to avoid committing this fallacy?

EXAMPLE:
Though Grant is a major in business management, he has taken several

courses with Professor Reynolds in the English Department because he greatly admires his teaching style and his expertise and scholarship in the classics. Because he likes Professor Reynolds, he is considering getting a minor in English. He belongs to a business fraternity and twice a semester their meetings are devoted specifically to a discussion of some social or political issue. The topic of this particular meeting is whether private businesses should have their own affirmative action programs or whether the government should require such programs. Grant said that he believes that private businesses will voluntarily have their own affirmative action programs so there's no need for any government regulation. When Fred asked him what his evidence was, Grant said, "My English professor, Dr. Reynolds, has said so on numerous occasions and he's so smart, he should know!"

EXERCISES:
1.   How would you explain to Grant that he has committed the fallacy of appeal to authority?
2.   How might Grant defend himself against the charge?

ACTIVITIES:
1.   Describe two commercials you have seen that involve a famous person advertising a particular brand of something, yet the person is not an authority on that type of product.
2.   Complete the following to illustrate the fallacy of appeal to authority and then complete it to illustrate a legitimate appeal to authority: "Decaffeinated coffee is better for you because..."

The Fallacy Of Appeal To Force

When rational discourse fails to persuade someone, it may be tempting to appeal to force to persuade the person. The "persuasive" nature of this fallacy takes on the appearance of "might makes right." While a threat may give the person a reason for changing his or her mind, appealing to force has no logical bearing on the acceptability of a position. Thus an appeal to force as a method of persuasion is fallacious.

EXAMPLE:
Mr. Williams was running for the office of mayor. During his campaign, he stopped to visit Ms. Johnson, who owns a construction company. He was hoping that she would campaign for him. But she refused because, she said, she disagreed with most of his stands on various issues. He told her, "Well, your company has received a considerable number of contracts from the city. If you don't campaign for me and I win the election, I will see to it that you don't get anymore contracts from this city!"

EXERCISES:
1. How does this example show that Mr. Williams' method of persuasion is fallacious?
2. If you were Mr. Williams, how might you try to persuade Ms. Johnson to campaign for you?

EXAMPLE:
Jody decided he didn't want to play football today. A group of his peers needed to have one more person to make a team. When Jody told the group that he didn't feel like playing today, one of the group shouted, "If you don't play today, I'll make sure you don't play with us when you want to!"

EXERCISES:
1. How is Jody's peer using force as a method of persuasion?
2. What might be a rational method of trying to convince Jody to play?

ACTIVITIES:
1. Find two examples in the news that illustrate the fallacy of appeal to force.
2. From your own personal experience, identify situations in which this fallacy was committed.

PHILOSOPHICAL PROBLEM SHEET #22

Tote That . . . But Where?

PROBLEM:

A hearing is being conducted by the Atomic Energy Commission (AEC) to determine by which route nuclear waste will be transported to a disposal site.

Certain sites have been approved for the disposal of nuclear wastes. The Allied Nuclear Corporation (ANC) has such a site near one of its nuclear power plants. Allied Nuclear wishes to ship waste from another plant they own to this disposal site. There are four possible routes using various transportation options to ship the wastes. One route runs through several small towns and one large city. The other route runs through a rural area near a couple of small towns. Both of these routes make use of a large truck. The truck which carries the nuclear waste must be identified through an easily readable sign stating that the truck is hauling nuclear waste. This is to warn people of possible dangers due to an accident. Another mode of transportation is a train. The train route runs through both rural and urban areas. Train tracks run from the plant which needs to dispose the nuclear waste to the disposal area. A final mode of transportation is the use of an airplane. There are airfields near both the plant and disposal area. The proposed route would take the plane over urban and rural areas at 30,000 feet.

The problem of nuclear waste has been an issue since the first nuclear power plant went into operation in the 1950's. Nuclear energy generates electrical power by creating steam which turns giant turbines. However, along with the power comes nuclear waste. The waste from a nuclear power plant is highly radioactive. The radioactive nuclear waste does not become harmless for thousands of years. Nuclear power companies have developed means to carry and dispose of waste which they hope will not harm mankind. The individuals who handle waste use protective clothing. The waste is sealed in metal casing and shipped to disposal sites far from populated areas. Environmentalists argue there is still great danger in nuclear wastes. Shipping could result in accidental leakage. When the waste is stored underground, leakage from the metal casing could result in ground water contamination. The nuclear power companies advocate the continued use of nuclear power. They argue that nuclear power is an excellent form of energy and cleaner than the burning of coal. They also argue that the nuclear power industry is working to minimize the waste danger to people. Presently, they must store the waste the best way they can. Both the urban and rural areas are aware of both the environmental and the nuclear industry's positions. However, they object to waste being shipped through their areas.

The urban group argues that shipping waste through urban areas could result in potentially dangerous consequences. The truck, train or plane could crash, rupturing the metal containment boxes carrying the waste. Although the containers are tested to withstand possible serious accidents, the spilling of waste is a possibility. The radiation from the waste could affect people by getting into drinking water or spreading through the air. Within an urban area many people could suffer or die. The urban group also says that terrorists could attack the various carriers and cause the above consequences. Terrorists could obtain information about the various shipments and make the waste transportation vehicles targets. Traveling late at night would help avoid traffic problems but other dangers would still exist. The urban group argues that a less heavily populated area would suffer fewer risks.

The rural group argues that even the smallest danger of something going wrong with the shipments is too great. People choose to live in rural areas to avoid the congestion of urban areas. Why should they be required to take risks urbanites refuse to take? The rural group maintains their rural location would make terrorism easier due to the amount of woods and open fields. They point out that a leak from the metal casings around the waste, whether by train, truck or plane, could contaminate the soil. Food comes from the soil. This contamination would affect people who eat this food throughout the land.

ACTIVITY:
You are a member of the AEC and must help decide what to do. You may vote in favor of the urban or rural group. You may also come up with an alternative solution. What you must do now is decide what position you would favor and which one(s) you would oppose. Please list your first choice and reasons for this choice. Also list your other choice(s) and give arguments why this/these would be undesirable options.

QUESTIONS:
1.   With what issue is the Atomic Energy Commission concerned?
2.   What are the possible methods of transporting the waste?
3.   What criteria or considerations would you establish concerning the

shipment of waste if you were a member of the Atomic Energy Commission?

4.   Assume, for the sake of argument, that the U.S. DEFINITELY needs nuclear power to meet its energy needs. It has been proposed that a nuclear power plant should be built near your hometown. Many people both near and far away will benefit from the power. However, your hometown runs the possible risk of contamination by a nuclear accident. Your town has decided to try to stop the building of the plant in court. What evidence should a judge consider before s/he makes a decision on whether to allow the construction of the plant?

5.   Should certain people be required to take risks for the betterment of the world? Why?

6.   Research both the pros and cons of nuclear power. From your research, decide whether you are pro- or anti-nuclear power. Present your position and reasons for your decision.

EXTENSION:

We live in a society in which there are risks. How do we assume which risks will be taken?

Individuals differ in their interpretation of which risks are acceptable. One may be afraid of flying while another feels safer in an airplane than driving long distances in a car. One person may feel safe with a chemical plant in town while another would move to avoid such a neighbor.

There are people who are opposed to nuclear power and in favor of coal-powered generators. Yet, thousands of miners have lost their lives in coal mines this century. The miners took risks which seem to be bearable to the advocates who do not have to undertake those risks.

We are now back to our first consideration: How do we decide what risks should be taken by society? This is a topic which could easily extend to the previous lesson. Some of the issues to be discussed are:

1.   Who determines what risks are acceptable? Is it an educated few or the mass of society?

2.   What kinds of information should be provided to individuals to help them decide which risks are worth taking?

3.   What roles do business and industry play in these decisions?

4.   Is there a set of guidelines which could be developed to act as rules for determining which risks are acceptable?

5.   Finally, what are acceptable risks?

PHILOSOPHICAL PROBLEM SHEET #23

How Do We Know What We Know?

How do we know what we know? Do we learn through our experiences? Do we intuitively know certain truths? Is rational thought more important than sense experiences in arriving at truth? Philosophers have thought through many of these questions. The following represent some schools of thought.

EMPIRICISM: The doctrine that the source of knowledge is experience and that all human knowledge is limited to the possible scope of human experience.

POSITIVISM: A philosophical theory which limits all knowledge to the scientifically verifiable.

RELATIVISM: The thesis that truth is relative to time, place, and group; there is no absolute and final truth.

RATIONALISM: The view that knowledge is to be tested not by sensory methods, but by deduction and reason.

INTUITIONISM: A source of knowledge which emerges from the subconsciousness without conscious intent.

All of the above can be utilized to help provide understanding about the world. However this does not mean that there is agreement over which particular method is best. Indeed a positivist might question whether a rationalist could arrive at the truth especially if knowledge or truth is limited to the "scientifically" verifiable. The rationalist might answer that Einstein's theory of relativity was formulated without the positivist method and is clearly accepted as a truth, which has been empirically proven.

Let's take the following example:

Thirty students at your high school have been assigned to a committee. This committee will try to determine methods which will reduce the amount of dropouts at the school. Determine how you seek these methods if you are a[n]:

1. Empiricist
2. Positivist
3. Relativist
4. Rationalist
5. Intuitionist

QUESTIONS:

1. How are each of these modes of knowledge different?
2. How might your path towards knowledge differ if you are an empiricist compared to a rationalist?
3. How might these methods work together?
4. Which of these modes would represent the scientific tradition?
5. Can you give examples of when science has made use of a combination of these methods to seek knowledge?
6. How might intuitionism be utilized in science?

EXTENSION:

How we determine which method to utilize when we problem solve is often a choice based on convenience. If we do not have time to orchestrate a study, we might simply sit down and think about an issue and hope for an acceptable solution. What is so interesting is that we jump from one particular mode to another depending on the situation and generally act on our decision. Hopefully it is a good decision!

Students generally enjoy telling about different ways they have come to knowledge or a solution to a particular issue. Indeed when I was young, I was convinced that teachers had eyes in the back of their heads. Why else could they always catch me? When I grew older and became a teacher, I realized that these eyes are based on a combination of empiricism, rationalism and intuitionism.

Parents oftentimes seem to have intuition when it involves their children. Indeed, some argue that in general, women are more intuitive than men! From past experience, my mother called twice during the evening after I had been injured in accidents. Her first question each time was, ''What's wrong?'' This is amazing since I was living five thousand miles away.

Have the students talk about these various modes of knowledge. A good exercise is to have the students analyze the media and government to see which mode of thought seems dominant in their pronouncements.

Another good exercise would be to have a theoretical scientist come talk to the class about how scientific theories are developed. This person could come from any variety of disciplines.

PHILOSOPHICAL ESSAY

Wide Reflective Equilibrium

BACKGROUND:

In our first three essays we have tried to point out how a person is able to reach commonality when developing moral principles, rules, and concepts. In Essay #1 we focused on moral objectivity and concluded that there can not be complete objectivity in morality; there will always be some reference to a person's attitudes, intuitions, and unreflective commitments. Yet, we still held out hope for objectivity in one form or another and suggested that whatever objectivity is realized will come through those who are committed to honest and open reflection; people who are willing to reconsider the values which they hold and then compare and revise these values as needed.

In Essay #2 we continued our dialogue by suggesting a definition of "morality" itself. It was suggested that two routes must be taken to understand this concept and its role in society. The first considered morals as deriving their meaning instrumentally; that is, functionally. A person, to define morality adequately, should consider the effects of a given moral judgment on other human beings, life forms, and the environment. The second route to discovering the meaning of morality was to simply acknowledge the innate and basic worth of human beings as a value in and of itself. We concluded that life has value or worth, not because of or for something else, but because it is life. This is an intrinsic definition of morality.

In Essay #3 the question was asked about the justification of morality. The question, "Why ought I be moral?" recognizes that some people are moral and some are not. This question keeps open the door of moral reflection and moral evaluation or justification. It is open to new understandings and demands relevant and revised explanations. The question reminds a person that morality is never complete; rather, it is an ongoing process.

This final essay will suggest a method of justification or evaluation that will be helpful as we explore with our students the very foundations of moral norms. This method is called "Wide Reflective Equilibrium." Although in its early stages of philosophical development, this method has the potential of rendering our moral intuitions and judgments in a coherent and objective fashion. Our goal remains providing an explanation for understanding. Moral thought, to be effective, should stand up to reflection. Even if the foundations of morality are known only intuitively — that life is value

— the consequences of that intuition lie only in justifying our dispositions to accept certain moral statements and act upon them.

How a person is to confirm the truthfulness of moral intuitions with reflection, self-understanding, and criticism, is a question that philosophy alone cannot answer. It is a question that will be answered through reflective living and is to be discovered as a result of a reasoning process which essentially cannot formulate the answer in advance. Philosophical understanding will play a role in this process, but it cannot provide the final and absolute answer for us. One must deliberate from personal experience, from a point of view that is first personal and then social.

WIDE REFLECTIVE EQUILIBRIUM:

So, how do we assist students with moral understanding? The answer is that we begin with what we have—our own pre-reflective judgments about what is right and what is wrong. Thus, we begin with our own ethical judgments or intuitions: Intuitions about the rightness or wrongness of some particular behavior and about certain general principles, such as "all human beings have a right to life," "one should try to keep one's promises," or "gratuitous cruelty to animals is wrong." People will have considered judgments at all levels of generality. They reflect and make judgments about particular situations, institutions, standards, and principles.

These considered judgments will always be open to revision. As such, they represent merely that starting point of coherent moral perspective. Still, a person must acknowledge that these starting points are historically, culturally, and personally relative. The weakness of the so-called "values-clarification" approach to morality is that it stops here. Values-clarification recognizes one's personal moral intuitions as the beginning and the ending of the valuing process. Hence, it fails to offer reflective justification, considering all values, because someone thinks they are true, equally significant.

Although our intuitions are relatively stable and represent widely shared perspectives, where intuitions are inconsistent internally or with recognized social and historical knowledge about human beings, or where intuitions conflict, a method of appraisal is needed.

Critics will say that a person's moral intuitions are learned at home, where what is taught is biased, unreflective, and inconsistent. Some will argue that many forms of morality are derived from religious systems, warped views of society, and/or from customs necessary for the survival of the group. They are neither culturally nor personally neutral. Because of this inner subjectivity, it is suggested that a person's moral intuitions be subjected to a wider reflection. This requirement tells one that what is needed is informed individuals with a wide variety of personal experiences.

The first step in the process of wide reflective equilibrium is to reconsider, compare and evaluate one's moral intuitions with other relevant and different moral theories. Secondly, one must take care that personal moral adjustments are internally consistent, and thirdly, they must take into account relevant information from both the social and human sciences. This final step will lead one outside of morality entirely to consider the effects of this reconsidered point of view as reflected in the objective knowledges of relevant sciences. It will aid a person in making moral judgments externally consistent with relevant information about humans and human environments.

Thus, although a person begins with personal intuitions and value judgments, the process of wide reflective equilibrium will provide a consistent filtering system to remove those points of view which are likely to be distorted. This process of moral adjustment and revision is necessary if one is ever to arrive at a coherent and objective moral perspective.

SUMMARY:

Finally, this reflective process will come to a close when reason and filtering tells a person that one moral judgment, one moral perspective, is to be rationally preferred to others. Instead of trying to squeeze moral principles from moral definitions, one must, in the final analysis, focus on the social nature and purposes of morality. By carefully considering the human and social function of a moral code—how it best can be fulfilled—a person may be able to advance reasonable and objective grounds for preferring some moral principles over others. This appears consistent with the regulatory function of morality—the evaluation and adjustment of human behavior. Any given morality is able to fulfill this function in a better or worse way, can satisfy or fail to satisfy one's aims in having moral connections in the first place. However, not all moral codes will perform equally well. This is why one must continually provide a basis for evaluating them.

PART THREE:
PLANNING &
TEACHING:
STRATEGIES FOR
IMPLEMENTING A
PRE-COLLEGE
PHILOSOPHY
CURRICULUM

A K-9 SEQUENTIAL PHILOSOPHY PROGRAM

There are many approaches to gifted education. Some schools have resource programs in which the students leave their classroom and then are homogeneously grouped from one to five hours a week for enrichment studies. The major thrust of these programs is to provide in-depth studies in subjects where the teacher has either an interest or background knowledge.

In other schools, the gifted are taught regular academic subjects at either a quicker rate or in more depth. Many times "in-depth" simply means that the students are being taught at a higher grade level. All the students in these classes may or may not be labeled "gifted." Some may be above average, but not gifted. Student groupings depend, to a large extent, on how the teacher is being paid—as either a regular classroom teacher or as a special education teacher.

There are some benefits to both types of programs, and the philosophy curriculum developed in this book can be used in either educational setting. The first type will be more flexible, but has the disadvantage of disrupting the normal schedule of the school. There will always be work to make up from missed classes. The second does not have this disadvantage, but is not as flexible in choice of subject matter.

The goals and objectives of gifted programs have largely been left to the creative imaginations and various academic preparations of the teachers of the gifted, the administrators who are responsible for establishing the program, or a few writers who have captured the market on gifted education. While yearly improvements in curricula for the gifted have been made, a different approach is genuinely needed. While some have been content with the way things are, there are others who have not only voiced their discontent but have undertaken the task of seeking improvement in curriculum materials. This book represents one of those undertakings.

While *Philosophy for Young Thinkers* is in no way intended to replace the creative and imaginative programs which teachers have developed and are now teaching, nor the individuality of the students in their care, it can be used as a GUIDE upon which programming and unit development can more consistently move.

There are some definite advantages for having a set of curricula guidelines:

1.   The requirement of writing IEP forms necessitates that the teacher identify annual goals, unit and learning objectives, methods and materials;

2.   The benefit of having a set of instructional objectives that can be used in whole or in part in any kind of program for the gifted;

3.   The knowledge that one's learning objectives are holistic in that they encompass the entire understanding continuum; and

4.   The awareness that you are expanding the student's knowledge of human behavior, physical background, values development, and productive thinking skills.

By using this approach, the teacher will be able to assist the student in discovering his or her own role in this process, thereby giving them the advantage of viewing the human situation with greater self-involvement and with a wider perspective.

CURRICULUM BREAKDOWN

The curriculum which is suggested for the academically gifted student focuses on the question, "What is human about humans?" The exploration of this question is organized around four conceptual schemes, each of which is further subdivided into three separate unit areas (see Chapters Four through Eight).

The purpose of this chapter is to relate this curriculum model to the various grades in the public schools. Next, we would like to suggest enrichment units and general learning objectives for each grade that both support and expand the Hester Curriculum Model (see Figure 9).

The enrichment units, general skills areas, and learning objectives suggested in Figure 9 will provide a way of including the Hester Curriculum Model in the curriculum for gifted students. Generally, the enrichment units that will be described below explore the dimensions of human identity and accept the idea that the public schools have an obligation to help students develop intellectually sound and ethically responsible answers to the most fundamental questions which gnaw at our society.

Each of the units in Figure 9 are designed to supplement the regular academic program in the classroom. In a resource program, these ideas can be expanded into more complete units for teaching and learning.

Figure 9 is divided into three different levels. LEVEL ONE is a Pre-Model Enrichment area which explores the concept of "self" in the personal, social, national and global worlds of the students. LEVEL TWO focuses on the Hester Model for the exploration of humanness and seeks to develop an integrated study of the question, "What is human about humans?" LEVEL THREE is a Post-Model Enrichment area which explores three areas of the study of humanness: the social, political, and moral perspectives.

The purpose of this curriculum breakdown is to provide a guide for implementing the study of humanness (and/or Philosophy) in grades K-12. The objectives of these units are:

1. To develop the creative and productive thinking skills of our very best students;

2. To help students acquire critical thinking skills in order to assimilate, process, and report a constant flow of information; and

3. To help students become UNDERSTANDING members of society.

ENRICHMENT UNITS

1. **Pre-Model Enrichment Units:**

    KINDERGARTEN: "ABOUT ME"
    In this enrichment unit the students will begin the process of exploring the different areas of their individuality. These areas include the students' physical make-up, personal skills, feelings, and values about self, others, and the world.

    Concepts included in this unit should include the following: interdependence, cooperation, social give-and-take, and personal identity. The young child should be encouraged to express feelings and ideas and to share them with the class to receive the reaction of others.

Curriculum areas such as physical education and health can support language arts and social studies explorations into personal identity.

The skills to be emphasized at this level are creative and productive thinking. The K-3 teacher should immerse her/himself in the works of Torrance, Guilford, Piaget, and Parnes.

GRADE ONE: "LIVING TOGETHER"
In this enrichment unit the students will explore ways in which people are alike and different. Consideration will be given to physical make-up, tastes, emotions, customs, values, and distinct ways of living. The students will begin to explore the nature of group life: play, work, school, and home.

Also, the students will look at the difference between city and rural life. They will explore how geographical differences produce cultural and individual differences. The same skills will be emphasized at this level as during the kindergarten years.

GRADE TWO: "THE WORLD IN WHICH WE LIVE"
In this enrichment unit the students will expand their knowledge of their social and geographical environments. Personal and local history are of prime importance to this study. The students will explore how the physical environment sets certain limits on how human beings live. Ecological issues such as clean water, air, and industrial pollution will be studied.

Brainstorming and problem-solving techniques should be used to discover the many ways the students think these problems can be solved.

Students will also learn how people have modified their environments through science and technology. Today's world should be compared with the world of their grandparents in order to bring the element of change into focus.

The teacher should use a variety of resources to highlight and add interest to this unit. Maps, graphs, and charts can be used in the assessment of problems. Movies and filmstrips add visual interest.

GRADE THREE: "EXPLORING INDIVIDUAL UNIQUENESSES"
In this enrichment unit the students will study the following aspects of their individuality: physical needs, emotional needs, physical appearance, abilities, feelings, tastes, and similarities and differences with other human beings.

The students will also explore the nature of their responsibility to self, family, community, country, and world. They will investigate the abilities of humans to create culture and will study such cultural components as technology, institutions, values, folkways, and attitudes. They will study the earth and learn about its life-support system. Then, they will probe the possibility of life on other planets.

GRADE FOUR: "ECONOMICS"
In this enrichment unit the students will explore two basic economic facts of their cultural environment:
1.   How goods and services are produced, and
2.   How are people in metropolitan areas and rural areas alike and how are they different?
    The students will focus on the following factors of production: labor, resources, capital, and technological change. The students will relate these factors to the wants and needs of people in their community and other selected areas of the world. The problems of hunger, energy, and their relationship to war and peace will be brought into focus.
    Historically, the students will study the industrial revolution of the 18th and 19th centuries. This study will focus on energy sources and technological developments and will be compared with the technological revolution that has occurred since 1945.

GRADE FIVE: "POLITICAL SCIENCE"
In this enrichment unit, the student will explore the structure and functions of the city, county, and state governments. The students will seek to discover why governments are needed, how they are formed, and what their function is.
    Included in this exploration is a study of why governments create laws and how laws are enforced. Field trips to local centers of government should be included in this unit and local officials should serve as support personnel to the teacher in and outside the classroom.
    This study will be coupled with an initial survey of the basic principles of both the Declaration of Independence and the United States Constitution. Laws establishing local and state governments will also be explored.

GRADE SIX: "GROUP LIFE"
In this enrichment unit the student will begin to put together the many concepts that have been learned about people living and working together. They will explore the following understandings:

1. That human beings shape their beliefs and behaviors not only by tradition, but by reacting to particular human problems and needs;
2. That cultural change can make life better or it can make life worse; that wisdom must be used to assess life as it progresses through space and time;
3. That all people live in social groups, learn to behave from these groups, and within these groups produce a culture with unique traits and characteristics;
4. That even though one's cultural patterns are unique in many ways, they are still patterns, and as such, have basic similarities (called cultural imperatives); and
5. That the interdependence of individuals and groups of individuals in complex societies serves as a reminder that we are one species: homo sapiens.

2. THE HESTER MODEL FOR INVESTIGATING HUMANNESS

The following three grades will spend their time in detailed exploration of the meaning of "humanness." This exploration, spread over a three-year period, can easily handle the four conceptual schemes outlined in Chapters Three–Six. Conceptual Scheme Two: The Self and Self-Awareness, will be spread over the three-year period with Conceptual Schemes One, Three, and Four being used during the 7th, 8th, and 9th grades consecutively.

GRADE SEVEN: "EMERGING HUMANITY"
In this enrichment unit the student will begin to answer the question "What is human about humans?" This study will begin by reviewing the biological and cultural contexts in which humanity has arisen. The student will learn that human life is a product of heredity and environment as well as social and cultural interaction. The student will learn that together these forces generate individual uniqueness and societal patterns.

Emphasis will be given to recent anthropological studies of our most ancient ancestors. Critical analysis will be offered of these theories, and the students will be stimulated to compare these studies with the teachings of various religious groups in their own communities.

While pursuing these knowledges, the student will become involved in understanding how the personality is formed. The student will pursue the idea that the behavior of persons is guided and organized by one's idea of "self."

The student will begin to explore answers to the following questions:

1. What is the nature of being a human?
2. Is human nature the result of free will or is it almost completely determined?

Answers to these questions can lead to many directions and open many avenues for research and study. Some directions to which these questions may lead are discussions of social deviance, crime, the XYY chromosome phenomenon, law, and punishment. Discussions of free will could take one into a study of world religions and various conceptions of deity.

GRADE EIGHT: "VALUES/MORAL THINKING"

In this enrichment unit, the student will develop a basis for evaluating personal, societal, and universal moral-values. As a basis for studying values, the student will continue the study of "self." The student will undertake an exploration of the social forces which enrich and promote self-development. The student will learn that a person's behavior is guided and organized by the idea of "self," that personality cannot be understood apart from social interaction, and that people are most effective when they are treated as free, responsible, and unique individuals.

The student will recognize that moral values are a distinct set of value statements which need rational support. Within this context, the student will begin to ponder the questions, "Who am I?" and "Why am I?" and then explore both positive and negative views of the self.

GRADE NINE: "KNOWLEDGE"

A continuation of problem-solving skills builds in this enrichment unit to an exploration of "how" and "what" a person can say that s/he KNOWS FOR SURE. Here the student will begin an exploration of the nature, sources, scope, and limitations of human knowledge.

The student will learn that "knowing" is a subjective process, the product of a self. Thus, the sources of human knowledge will be discovered in the affective process of being a human being.

The student will define "truth" and "fact" and then relate them in a definition of "knowledge." The student will then use this definition in the search for OBJECTIVITY.

This study will be applied to (1) the search for the "self," (2) the meaning of "God," and (3) the clarification of the methods of science compared with those of religion.

Application of this study will come in the development of higher-level, critical thinking abilities such as concept formation, interpretive skills, and the development and support of hypotheses.

3.   **POST-MODEL IN-DEPTH EXPLORATIONS:**

The purpose of the enrichment units for grades ten through twelve is to give in-depth exploration to several of the key problems initiated by prior philosophical explorations. These are (1) the development of personality, (2) comparative political systems, and (3) moral responsibility.

GRADE TEN: "PERSONALITY & THE SOCIAL PERSPECTIVE"
Course Outline:
I.   What is Social Science?
    1.   Cultural Anthropology
    2.   Sociology
    3.   Social Psychology
    4.   Political Science
    5.   Economics
II.   What is the Scientific Method?
    1.   General Characteristics
    2.   The Research Process
    3.   Sociological Inquiry
    4.   The Concept of "Social Fact"
III.   Culture, Society, and Personality
    1.   The Nature and Functions of Culture
    2.   Social Organization and Interaction
    3.   Personality and Social Interaction
    4.   Deviance and Social Change
IV.   Social Institutions
    1.   The Family
    2.   Religion
    3.   Education
    4.   Government

GRADE ELEVEN: "COMPARATIVE POLITICAL SYSTEMS"
Course Outline:
I.   Introduction

       1.   Leadership and Institutions
       2.   Decision-Making
       3.   The Role of Individuals in Society
       4.   The Function, Variations, and Changes in Government
  II.   The Political Systems of Several Primitive Societies
       1.   The American Cheyenne
       2.   The San Blas Cuna of Panama
       3.   The Tupi Indians of Brazil
 III.   The United States and the U.S.S.R.
       1.   Democracy
       2.   Totalitarianism
       3.   Federalism
       4.   Socialism
       5.   Communism
 IV.   Models of Social Order
       1.   Order from Science
       2.   Order from Reason
       3.   Order from God
       4.   Order from Power
       5.   Order from the Market
       6.   Order from Conflict

GRADE TWELVE: "MORAL RESPONSIBILITY"
Course Outline:
   I.   What is Responsibility?
  II.   The Self
       1.   The Self and Society
       2.   The Self as Decision-Maker
       3.   The Self as Consciousness
       4.   The Self and Others
 III.   Reason and Method
       1.   Ethics and Reason
       2.   Moral Validation
       3.   Scientific Validation
       4.   The Method of Moral Judgment
 IV.   Responsibility and Freedom
       1.   The Nature of Freedom
       2.   Freedom and Choice
       3.   Determination
       4.   Autonomy

V.   Moral Responsibility
   1.   Humans as Moral Agents
   2.   Responsibility or Answerability
   3.   Condemnation
   4.   Punishment

Only the bare framework has been suggested for unit and course work. It will be left to the creative abilities and academic preparations of the teachers of gifted students to organize these enrichment units and conceptual schemes into usable classroom curricula. This chapter and those prior to it are written for the purpose of giving direction to many of our educational yearnings for in-depth direction.

PURPOSE, FOCUS, AND UTILIZATION

Philosophy was not always philosophy. The word "philosophy" has repeatedly changed its meaning. "Philosophy" and "philosophical man" are expressions to be found for the first time in Heraclitus around 504-501 B.C. One of his aphorisms runs: "Philosophical men, namely, shall have knowledge of a great many things." Strangely enough, coinciding with modern usage, "philosopher" means a person searching for ultimate truth. Apart from this solitary instance, however, "philosophy" was originally equivalent to "science," "research," "intelligence," "education," "intellectual culture," "mathematics," "geometry," "wisdom," and "the art of sensible conduct in life."

Actual modern usage distinguishes *theoretical philosophy* and *practical philosophy*. Although their purposes are different, the two fields have much in common; for example, the development of certain intellectual and reasoning skills. The purpose of theoretical philosophy consists of constructions, conclusions, conceptions, hypotheses, and theories. Its goal is that of creating a consistent world picture.

On the other hand, practical philosophy's goal is to teach people how to live a sensible life. This is what is called "moral" or "ethical" philosophy. Theoretical philosophy is the art of speculation, practical philosophy is the art of living. One focuses on the construction of world hypotheses, the other, on how to live reasonably by ethical standards.

The *Philosophy For Young Thinkers Program* is an effort in developing a practical program in philosophy at the pre-college level. This does not mean that the skills necessary for theoretical philosophy are being ignored. To the contrary, *Philosophy for Young Thinkers* places a great deal of emphasis on the same skills needed for theoretical philosophy. Skills such as inductive and deductive reasoning patterns, the assessment of the credibility of statements of fact, problem-solving, and the like are as necessary for the development of practical reason as they are for theoretical reason. Although the goals of these two areas are generically different, the critical thinking skills and reasoning processes for completing their individual purposes are the same. Both of these areas seek explanations and understandings of reality, ideas, concepts and conclusions.

In his book, *Philosophical Explanations*, Robert Nozick says that "explanation increases understanding." Indeed it does for explanations represent our efforts to organize experiences and make rational our thoughts and behaviors. On the other hand, understanding tells us what is impossible. As we organize our experiences and make our thoughts and behaviors more rational, our understandings of human possibility becomes clearer and clearer to us.

Nozick's analysis reveals the very purpose of thinking as "explanation for understanding." This is rational thinking. The contrary to rationality, irrationality, appears confused, chaotic, and purposeless. The application of rational thinking can be made in both theoretical and practical philosophy. This application includes, but is not limited to, the rational processes of inductive thinking, deductive thinking, the scientific method, thinking involving moral arguments, and problem-solving.

Behind these rational processes stands a network of skills which we have come to know as "thinking skills." The development of thinking skills is a prerequisite to the mastering of the above mentioned rational processes. The Cognitive/Affective Skills Chart included in this chapter provides for the teacher a sequential list of thinking skills organized and divided by grade level. They fall under the headings of Research Skills, Thinking Skills and Creativity Skills (RTC).

At the heart of being able to think at higher levels of critical reason is the ability to make inferences. As people have experiences, these experiences are translated by the mind into internal symbols. In turn, these internal symbols are related to other internal symbols (the knowledge and organization of past experiences) and afterwards retranslated into actions (behaviors).

This inferential process represents a continual movement, back and forth, from thought to word and to thought to behavior. The ability of persons to manipulate their internal representations of experience and act upon them is necessary for the development of higher level thinking skills and reasoning processes on both practical and theoretical philosophy. This is philosophical understanding.

In this chapter we will outline the program which we are now writing in pre-college philosophy. This book represents only an introduction to that program. It provides program purposes, goals, and objectives. It gives a rationale for the development of activities and curriculum at higher levels of thinking for gifted students. Beginning in the primary years, we are offering a program which focuses on both conceptual and critical thinking skills development leading up to the ability to employ reasoning networks in the decision-making process. *Philosophy For Young Thinkers* is a curriculum for young people. It provides an opportunity for mental growth and maturity. It engages the young student's attention through stories, cartoons, and—for the very young—hands on activities.

K-3 Elementary Philosophy Curriculum
Getting Acquainted With Philosophy

   (Teacher's Guide To K-3 Program)
   (K)   About Me
   (1)   Living Together
   (2)   My Expanding World
   (3)   But, I'm Different

Purpose:
The purpose of the *K-3 Getting Acquainted With Philosophy Program* is the introduction of the young child to the mental habits and important concepts/ideas which are necessary for a lifetime of successful learning and creative problem-solving.

Focus:
The focus of this program is both cognitive and affective. The cognitive focus of the K-3 Program is the skills of *research* (observing, collecting and describing data, comparing and classifying, finding new relationships, and looking for assumptions): *thinking operations* (identifying facts, listing, matching, looking for sameness and difference, sequencing, making verbal distinctions, and understanding cause/effect conclusions); and *creativity* (developing curiosity about the self and others, learning to brainstorm, and evaluating ideas and conclusions).

   The affective emphasis of this program focuses on the development of concepts, attitudes, and behaviors. The basic interest is in practical philosophy which stresses the following human concepts: the *self* (including self-awareness, patience, self-confidence, and positive attitudes); *others* (including receptiveness, respect, appreciation, and understanding of others); and *connectedness* (including the acceptance of others and self, time-span relationships, responsibility to nature, and responsibility to others).

Utilization:
The skills and concepts in this program are sequentially related and developmentally organized so that the teacher—at any level—can effectively utilize them. The Cognitive/Affective Skills Chart at the end of this chapter shows the relationship of each of these processes to each other. At any grade level, the teacher—working vertically with this chart—will be able to use a set of cognitive skills (research, thinking, creativity) and a set of affective concepts (self, others, connectedness) with each grade level. Each grade level activity book will focus on one set of these cognitive skills and affective concepts and provides twenty one activities to assist the teacher with their reinforcement. A teacher's guide is provided for each set of activity books, and it gives additional information on how to teach pre-college philosophy and introduce abstract concepts and higher level thinking skills to young people.

On the following pages is a sample lesson from the *K-3 Getting Acquainted With Philosophy Program*. This lesson is from the Kindergarten manual and will give you some insights on how we have approached the teaching of this material to very young children.

- -

Lesson Guide: About Me
Level: Kindergarten

Willie The Worm

Instructions:
Before using "Willie The Worm" with your class, look over the materials and activities list for ideas to further enrich and extend this lesson. Motivate your students to learn by making this and other lessons colorful, interesting and relevant.

The teacher should tell or read the story of "Willie" to the class. A puppet of a worm could be used to enhance the story. The teacher could use this puppet as the story is told to capture the interest of the young students. Also, a student could be selected to work the puppet.

Create a "Willie The Worm" bulletin board before the exercise begins. Let the students help with this project. On the bulletin board construct a huge "Willie" with a gigantic heart. Beside Willie place the following question: "What does it mean to have a big heart?" This is a lead-in discussion question which will be used later on.

Have the children imagine how a worm would sound if it could talk. How would a fat one sound? a skinny one? a short one? or a long one? Give all the children a chance to participate in this exercise.

Materials Needed:
[1]   Socks to make "Willie" puppets.
[2]   Egg cartons, pipe cleaners, chenile balls, felt, buttons, needle and thread for puppet variations.
[3]   Construction paper of different colors.
[4]   Scissors and glue.
[5]   Various colors of paint.

Extension Activities:
[1]   Students can construct their own Willie Worms out of construction paper, egg cartons and chenile balls, pipe cleaners, or socks.
[2]   These Willie Worms can be given to people whom the students like. Make sure that Willie has a big, big heart.
[3]   Some of these Willie Worms can be placed on the bulletin board with a sample of the students' responses to the discussion questions.
[4]   The class can also use these puppets to put on a puppet show for the class or another class.

Lesson:
"Howdy pals! My name is Willie The Worm. My friends tell me that I have a big heart. Do you know what it means to have a big heart? . . . Well, that's just great! And I agree, because—to me—having a big heart means that I care about the feelings of other people.

Some people think that a person needs to be "grown-up" to have a big heart. Do you think that a person must be grown-up to have a big heart? . . . I agree with you. I believe that all people, big and small, young and old, can have big, big hearts, don't you?

Would you like to tell Willie why you have a big heart? Look at the bulletin board. Do you see my picture? Do you see my big, big heart? Would you like to share with the class your ideas about what it means to have a big heart?"

Questions:
[1]   What does it mean to have a big heart?
[2]   Does Willie have a big heart?
[3]   Do you have a big heart?
[4]   How do you feel when your heart is big?
[5]   Why is it hard to always have a big heart?

[6]   What do you do when your heart is big?
[7]   How can we help other people have big, big hearts?

Grades 4-6 Elementary Philosophy Curriculum
Philosophical Inquiry Program

(Teacher's Guide to 4-6 Program)
(4)   The Human Community
(5)   The Great Experiment
(6)   The Global Village

Purpose:
The purpose of the *4-6 Elementary Philosophical Inquiry Program* is the introduction of the elementary thinker to the skill of philosophical inquiry as it relates to the values and concepts inherent in the ethical community (either local, national, or worldwide.)

Focus:
The focus of this program is both cognitive and affective. The cognitive focus of the 4-6 Program is the inquiry method of problem-solving and the skills needed for this process. The inquiry process treats students as investigators. Using the method of discovery, students are to use inductive evidence to generate relevant solutions to the problems which are being confronted.

The cognitive focus of this program includes the skills of *research* (hypothesizing, explaining, collecting and organizing data, interpreting and evaluating information); *thinking operations* (imagining and drawing conclusions, the application of data and experimentation); and *creativity* (the use of creative written and oral expressions and the application of a global values orientation).

The affective emphasis of this program focuses on the development of concepts, attitudes, and behaviors. The basic interest is in practical philosophy which stresses the following fundamental concepts: *the self* (including the examination of beliefs and values, a willingness to share one's beliefs and values with others, and the development of goals for responsible self-growth); *others* (including the evaluation of important people, places, and things, the appreciation of the value of social institutions, and an understanding of social responsibility); *connectedness* (including the development of values toward others, and awareness of the need for human and environmental ethics, and the development of respect for individual differences).

Utilization:

The skills and concepts in this program are sequentially related and developmentally organized so that the teacher—at any grade level—can effectively utilize the program. The Cognitive/Affective Skills Chart at the end of this chapter shows the relationship of each of these processes to each other. At any grade level, the teacher—working vertically with this chart—will be able to use a set of cognitive skills and a set of affective concepts with each grade level. Each grade level activity book will focus on one set of these cognitive skills and affective concepts and provides twenty-one activities to assist the teacher with their reinforcement.

The *Grades 4-6 Teacher's Guide* provides background on how to use the inquiry method, teaching conceptually, reasoning skills and the gifted, and gives an overview of each activity book. It gives to the teacher additional information on teaching philosophy at the elementary level and introduces abstract concepts and higher level thinking skills to young people.

On the following pages is a sample lesson from the *Grades 4-6 Elementary Philosophical Inquiry Program*. This lesson is from the fourth grade manual and will give you some insights on how we have approached the teaching of this material for the elementary student.

Lesson Guide: The Human Community
Level 4

Rules For Living Together

Skills:
Explaining, Drawing Conclusions

Concepts:
Evaluation of rules of societal living
Examination of social norms and rules

Instructional Objectives:
The student will.
[1]   Explain the difference between a norm and a rule.
[2]   State the purpose of rules in a society.
[3]   Understand that norms and laws represent a society's values about good and bad behavior.

Procedures:

The teacher will . . .

[1]   Review with students the concepts of "social group" and "family" learned in previous lessons.
[2]   Share with students the objectives of this lesson.
[3]   Review inquiry situation with student.
[4]   Engage students in oral and written activities.

Questions For Inquiry Clarification:

[1]   Why did the Pilgrims, sign the Mayflower agreement?
[2]   Can you explain the concept of "direct democracy?"
[3]   What is the difference between direct and representative democracy?
[4]   Can you explain how a norm is an unwritten rule?
[5]   Why do societies write laws and enforce them?
[6]   In your home do you have norms and rules, or both?
[7]   Have you ever been punished for breaking a rule?
[8]   What would life be like without rules to guide our behavior?

Inquiry Situation:

Before the Pilgrims left the Mayflower, they signed an agreement to obey the government that they were about to set up in the new world. After landing in America, those who signed the Mayflower agreement were permitted to vote on new laws as these laws were needed in the community. Because each citizen got a vote on all community matters, the form of government they established was called "direct democracy."

Today, you and I live in social groups much like the Pilgrims. Some of these groups are small, like our families and clubs, and some are quite large, like our school, or even larger, like our state and nation. Every social group, large or small, has rules to guide it. These rules represent ways we expect each other to behave. For example, rules of the highway tell us how to drive our cars and how we should expect other people to drive their cars.

But some rules are not written down. These rules are typically called "norms." Our parents expect "good" behavior from us at home and when we are away from home. We know in our minds how we expect our friends to treat us. The problem is that people often surprise us—that is, they do the unexpected. When this happens frequently, we realize that this person does not understand or has not been taught the basic norms about getting along in a society of people. What they need are stronger rules. This is why your school writes its rules in a student handbook and why the state has laws to regulate our behavior.

Many people still break these rules. They even break laws. They fight, speed in cars, cheat on tests, and take drugs. When people continually break rules or laws they are punished by their society. It may be their family, their school, or their state that does the punishing, but when they get caught they do get punished.

Rules and norms are made to help us live a good life. Do you think rules and norms are necessary? Do you believe they make it easier for members of a group to get along with each other? What would life be like without rules and norms to guide us? Would all people be honest? helpful? truthful? What do you think?

Examples: Rule - You must go to church on Sunday.
Norm - My family believes in God and church.
Rule - You must not cheat on tests at school.
Norm - Our society puts a great deal of emphasis on being honest and truthful.

Activities:
−A− Norms and Rules:
[1] Make a list of three or four norms (unwritten rules) at your school or in your classroom.
[2] Make a list of three norms in your family.
[3] Take the norms in list #1 and #2 and rewrite each one as a rule for individual behavior. For each of these rules, create a punishment for those who break it.
[4] In a small group, discuss your list of norms, parallel rules, and resultant punishments. Can your group reach agreement on a consistent set of such norms, rules, and punishments? Explain.
[5] Did people in your group disagree because their norms are different from your norms? Explain.

−B− Rules and Norms:
[1] If your class or school has written rules, provide a copy for class members to read.
[2] For each class or school rule create a consistent norm. Read these aloud and discuss with the whole class. Did you find differences of opinion?
[3] Write these norms on the board. Divide the class into small groups of three or four students. Have each group answer: "Do you agree that these are norms about which all people are in agreement?" Each group is to state its reasons for its conclusions.

[4]   Have each group report its answers to the class. Do all students agree? Why? Why not?

[5]   Find out if other students in the school agree by interviewing them or completing a school survey. Report your findings to all who were involved.

RULES FOR LIVING TOGETHER
(Lesson Break Down)

- -

Lesson One:

[1]   Review with students the importance of the family and living up to one's family responsibilities as stated in the previous lessons.

[2]   State objective #1 to your class.

[3]   Go over "Inquiry Situation" with the class.

[4]   Engage students in activities A.1., A.2., and A.3.

[5]   Divide class into small groups and have each group complete activities A.4. and A.5.

[6]   While in their groups, have students share reasons, justify (give reasons for) their reasons, and write down their reasons.

[7]   Each group is to report their efforts to the class as a whole. Their purpose is not to reach a solution but to raise further questions about norms and rules. During the class discussions, clarify questions, raise specific issues, examine ideas and the consequences suggested by the students.

[8]   Bring discussion to a close in the class by summarizing the efforts of your students and creating a poster (to be placed in the class) which contains the summary.

Note: This lesson will take more than one class period.

- -

- -

Lesson Two

[1]   Review with students the findings of Lesson One.

[2]   Review objectives #2 and #3 with students.

[3]   Engage students in activities B.1. – B.5.

[4]   Bring this lesson to a close by completing a school survey (or have students interview a specific number of other students) about rules and norms.

[5] Possible ways of bringing lesson to a conclusion:
   (a) Summarize school survey and/or interviews and make a written report of summary. Distribute to all students/classes involved.
   (b) Have each student in the class write one example of someone obeying a school rule and one example of someone breaking that same rule.
   (c) Have students write a scenario of someone who is confused about a certain rule and what happens to this person. Read these aloud in the class.

Middle Grades Philosophy Curriculum
Philosophical Problem-Solving Program

(Teacher's Guide to Middle Grades Program)
(MG.   1.)   Human Configurations
(MG.   2.)   Beat Him When He Sneezes
(MG.   3.)   Wrong-Think/Non-Think

Purpose:
The purpose of the *Middle Grades Philosophical Problem-Solving Program* is to introduce middle grades students to the skill of philosophical problem-solving as it relates to their growing awareness of the human environment with all of its positive and negative connotations.

Focus:
The focus of this program is both cognitive and affective. The cognitive focus of the Middle Grades Program is the problem-solving method, especially as it relates to serious human problems, and its concomitant skills. The problem-solving process permits students to solve problems individually or in small groups. Of great importance to this process is the ethical or moral evaluation of conclusions and solutions prior to acting upon them.

The cognitive focus of this program includes the skills of *research* (the scientific method, logical thinking, and emphasizing analysis, synthesis, and evaluation); *critical thinking* (focusing on the method of philosophical problem-solving); and *creativity* (emphasizing the development of mental flexibility and elaboration as it comes to bare on the decision-making process).

The affective emphasis of this program focuses on the development of concepts, attitudes, and behaviors. The basic interest is in practical philosophy which stresses the following fundamental concepts: *the self* (including creating goals for self-development, the establishing of criteria for judging behavior, and the rational support of ideas and beliefs); *others* (including identifying those who give meaning to one's life, consistency in moral decision-making, and the development of respect for the "personhood" of others); and *connectedness* (including becoming sensitive to the necessity of other life forms, understanding the relationship between personal, social, and universal values, and the exploration of the relationship between different kinds of knowing).

Utilization:
Like the Primary and Elementary programs, the skills and concepts in this series are sequentially related and developmentally organized so that the teacher can effectively utilize these lessons. Each grade level activity book will focus on one set of skills and concepts and provides twenty-one activities for classroom use.

Lesson Guide: Beat Him When He Sneezes
Middle Grades, Book 2

A Shattered Innocence

Skills:
Analysis, evaluation

Concepts:
Establishing a criteria for judging behavior. Becoming more consistent in moral decision-making.

Instructional Objectives:
The student will. . .
[1] Understand the nature of a moral decision.
[2] Be able to explain the relationship between responsibility and morality; responsibility and reason.

Procedures:
The teacher will. . .
[1] Review with students the concept of morality and the process of moral reasoning.
[2] Share with students the objectives of this lesson.

[3] Review inquiry situation with students.

[4] Engage students in oral and written activities.

Questions For Inquiry Clarification:

[1] What do we mean by the word ''moral?''

[2] Why should human beings be moral?

[3] Can you give reasons for being moral?

[4] If you can give reasons for being moral, does this mean that you are responsible for your actions?

[5] Under what conditions are people not responsible for their actions?

[6] Can businesses and industries be held morally responsible for their business practices or for what they manufacture?

Inquiry Situation:

Headlines: "ASTRONAUTS' VULNERABILITY UNMASKED, '84 Shuttle Crew Absorbing Shock of Space Program's Demolished Image of Infallibility"

Before the unthinkable happened on that cold January day in Florida, they were the elite's elite, operating in that strange, unforgiving stratosphere where only several hundred humans have ever been.

With space flight becoming virtually routine, the astronauts came to be seen as near flawless as robots. The explosion of the space shuttle Challenger on January 28, 1986, changed all that.

As one middle school student remarked: ''I didn't think that spaceflight was all that dangerous. I thought it was just another job.'' In one single tragic moment, all of that was changed. Now the astronauts have suddenly become as fragile and vulnerable as earthbound mortals.

In the grief, confusion, and anger that followed the tragic explosion, the shuttle program lost its innocence. After a four month investigation, a presidential commission concluded the catastrophe was ''an accident rooted in history,'' that is, NASA's acceptance of growing risks in trying to meet an increasingly ambitious schedule. As astronaut Capt. Frederick Hauck said: ''Although the technical problems were coming faster than the solutions, the launch dates remained firm. Then, Challenger exploded.''

Hauck went on to remark, ''Morals were not involved in the Challenger accident. I don't think anyone willingly subverted the system within NASA.''

The question of moral responsibility is an important question. It's a question which you and I confront almost everyday and a question which we wish we could ignore. The curse of men is that they know of good and evil.

Whether they will or not, men will be judged as moral agents, and condemned for their failures. Men know too much to be considered as innocent as beasts of the fields.

Although astronaut Hauck believes morals are not an issue in the Challenger's explosion because no one personally and willingly subverted the system, are not the businesses that men run accountable for their actions and their inactions? Human life is a burden of moral responsibility.

For example, in the aftermath of the Challenger's accident, the astronauts have been especially angered by the revelation that they were kept in the dark about the unreliability of the O-rings in the solid rocket boosters. They agreed that there is no such thing as zero risk in the space business, but they felt that they should have been informed about the risks, whatever that might be, so that they could have made their own decisions about flying. Was NASA acting immorally when it downplayed the O-ring danger and took an inherent life endangering decision out of the hands of those whose lives were in danger?

Activities:

[1]   There are two senses of moral responsibility:

    (a)   Pervasive responsibility is the sense that, as human beings, we are responsible for every human event—good or bad. Also, pervasive responsibility means that we ought to rid the world of all evil, but it does not imply that we can so rid the world. We may not have the means to perform such an act. The world cannot be confronted in detail at every turn, yet, we must face the world morally, choosing and acting on our choices.

    (b)   Personal responsibility, on the other hand, implies that we can praise and blame a person for their actions. Here, a person is personally responsible for an action which is uniquely his or hers, which cannot be laid to anyone else's responsibility. Here, ought does imply can.

[2]   Have students reconsider the idea of moral responsibility. Give them the above two definitions and ask them to. . .

    (a)   restate the two senses of moral responsibility in their own words.

    (b)   give examples of both senses of moral responsibility.

[3]   Present the Inquiry Situation to the students, then have students. . .

    (a)   Classify the ignoring of the O-ring danger by NASA as either a pervasive or a personal responsibility and state reasons for classification.

(b) Develop—in a small group of three students—a research project on the Challenger disaster. Let each group reach its own conclusions about responsibility in the matter and whether any one person or group is to blame for the explosion.

(c) Reconsider—while each group makes it report to the class—all evidence in terms of moral blame and moral praise.

Then have the class discuss answers to the following questions:

1. Was the disaster a result of immoral behavior?

2. Can you give reasons for your answers?

[4] The class may want to find out how other students feel about the Challenger disaster. Permit them to survey others in the school about their feelings. Report findings to the class.

A Shattered Innocence
(Lesson Breakdown)

- -

Lesson One:

[1] Review with students the concept of values and moral values.

[2] State Objectives #1 and #2 to the class.

[3] Involve students in completing activities [1] and [2].

[4] Close class by listening to students' examples of the two senses of responsibility and making sure that the students are clear about the nature of each.

- -

Lesson Two:

[1] Review findings and knowledge learned in Lesson One with the class.

[2] Restate objective #2 to the class.

[3] Using Questions for Clarifications, solicit answers from the class in a general discussion.

[4] Close the period by summarizing the answers given and agreed upon by the class to these questions.

- -

Lesson Three:

[1] Review the findings of Lesson Two with class.

[2] Restate Objective #2 to the class.

[3] Share inquiry situation with class.

[4] With class, work to complete activities [3] and [4].

[5] Bring lesson three to a close by asking students to give their gut feeling about the shuttle disaster after going through a lesson on moral responsibility.

- -

COGNITIVE/AFFECTIVE SKILLS CHART: K-12

K-3
COGNITIVE SKILL DEVELOPMENT

K	1	2	3
Research Skills:			
Observing: Collecting Describing	Comparing Classifying	Finding new relationships	Looking for assumptions
Thinking Skills:			
Identifying Listing Matching	Looking for: Sameness Difference	Sequencing: making verbal distinctions	Understanding: cause/effect conclusions
Creativity Skills:			
Development of curiosity about self	Development of curiosity about others	Learning to brainstorm	Brainstorming, Producing ideas Evaluation

K-3
AFFECTIVE CONCEPTUAL DEVELOPMENT

K	1	2	3
Toward the Self:			
Self-Awareness	Patience	Self-Confidence	Positive Attitudes
Toward Others:			
Receptiveness	Respect	Appreciation	Understanding
Connectedness:			
Acceptance	Time-span relations	Responsibility to Nature	Responsibility to others

GRADES 4-6
COGNITIVE SKILL DEVELOPMENT

4	5	6
Research Skills:		
Hypothesizing	Hypothesizing	Interpreting information
Explaining	Explaining	Evaluating information
	Collecting and	
	Organizing Data	
Thinking Skills:		
Imagining and drawing conclusions	Application and Experimentation	Application and Experimentation
Creativity Skills:		
Creative written and oral expression	Creative written and oral expression	Global values orientation

GRADES 4-6
AFFECTIVE CONCEPTUAL DEVELOPMENT

4	5	6
Toward the Self:		
Examination of beliefs and values	Willingness to share beliefs and values with others	Development of goals for responsible growth
Toward Others:		
Evaluation of important people, places, and things	Appreciation of the value of social institutions	Defines the meaning of social responsibility
Connectedness:		
Development of values toward others	Becomes aware of the need for human and environmental ethics	Respect and value individual differences

GRADES 7-9
COGNITIVE SKILL DEVELOPMENT

7	8	9
Research Skills:		
Scientific Method	Analysis Synthesis Evaluation	Logical Thinking
Thinking Skills:		
Problem-Solving	Problem-Solving	Problem-Solving
Creativity Skills:		
Development of flexibility and elaboration	Development of flexibility and elaboration	Decision-Making

GRADES 7-9
AFFECTIVE CONCEPTUAL DEVELOPMENT

7	8	9
Toward the Self:		
Create goals for self development	Establish criteria for judging behavior	Give beliefs rational support
Toward Others:		
Identify those who give meaning to life	Be consistent in moral decision-making	Respect the effort of others to make their ideas known
Connectedness:		
Become sensitive to the necessity of other life forms	Understand the relationship between personal, social, and universal values	Explore the relationship between different kinds of knowing

GRADES 10-12
COGNITIVE SKILL DEVELOPMENT

10	**11**	**12**
Research Skills:		
Relating, comparing, explaining, evaluating	Distinguishing, hypothesizing, logically supporting	Interpreting, arguing rationally
Thinking Skills:		
Future Problem-Solving	Future Problem-Solving	Future Problem-Solving
Creativity Skills:		
Creative Decision-Making	Creative Decision-Making	Creative Decision-Making

GRADES 10-12
AFFECTIVE CONCEPTUAL DEVELOPMENT

10	**11**	**12**
Toward the Self:		
Understand and develop individual uniquenesses	Clarify idea of self in relation to social institutions	Express and evaluate personal and social values
Toward Others:		
Form effective social relationships	Creative positive attitudes toward others	Develop a set of rules for moral growth and development
Connectedness:		
Explore the relationship of the self to others	Explore the development of social institutions	Relate moral growth and development to biological development

FIGURE 9

10 THE TUTTLE AG EXPERIENCE

INTRODUCTION

Establishing a program for gifted students is no easy matter. For a gifted program to become effective it needs to receive the commitment of the district superintendent and the district office staff; the commitment of the school principal; and the cooperation of the other teachers in the school. Most parents will be supportive of the teacher's efforts in setting up a gifted program, but an effective program demands consistent communication with parents as the program unfolds and is maintained over the years.

Also, an effective gifted program will have clear ideas about program dimensions, goals and objectives, and teaching methodologies. Parents, other teachers, and administrators will be interested in the development of the program, where and how monies are being spent, and the effect of the curriculum on gifted students. Gifted programs, despite efforts to keep all things normal and well-oiled, are high profile. People are interested in what is being taught and the methodologies being employed. Administrators are interested in getting the largest possible return for their monies. Principals are interested in quality teaching and maintaining parental communication. Gifted education can be an exciting adventure, but can also be exhausting and time consuming.

When done right, creating effective programs for the gifted is a difficult and high-energy (demanding) process. There are responsibilities other than teaching—to parents, other teachers, principals, and the central office staff. There are legal records to maintain and audits to withstand. Finally, there are the students, the reasons for the program.

This chapter outlines a program which we assisted in establishing at C. H. Tuttle Middle School in Catawba County, North Carolina. In North Carolina the state legislature demanded that all schools would have gifted programs in place by the fall of 1978. We began working with the program in 1977. The first few years were experimental, but gradually a curriculum (described in this chapter) emerged. As the parameters of the curriculum became more clearly defined, we were able to work with the principal and staff of the school to add other dimensions to the program which provides an enrichment area for students and a helpful dimension with regard to the other teachers in the school, assisting them with student research and enrichment activities.

The goal of the AG (academically gifted) Program at C. H. Tuttle Middle School is to improve the quality of basic schooling for those students who enter into the gifted classes. For this purpose several theoretical models have been combined to provide a program framework of holistic educational experiences. These theoretical models include the Paideia Proposal for Educational Reform developed by Mortimer Adler and his associates at the University of Chicago; the Renzulli Triad Model developed by Joseph Renzulli and his staff at the University of Connecticut; the Future Problem-Solving Program developed by E. Paul Torrance and maintained by the Torrance Center for Creative Studies at the University of Georgia; and *Philosophy for Young Thinkers*, a program being written by Joseph P. Hester and Philip F. Vincent.

The Paideia Proposal was an exciting discovery because it recognizes the pluralistic nature of the public school and presents a curricula framework within which a variety of curricula can be soundly constructed, appropriate to the particular circumstances and needs of different students. Although the Paideia Program was not written for gifted students *per se*, we found that it offered an adequately researched trilogy of goals, methodologies, and content areas of operation (see: Table #1).

The Future Problem-Solving Program fits nicely into the Paideia Proposal as a developmental skills emphasis which involves and excites students with real problems and the training in the necessary skills to solve them. We found that the Future Problem-Solving Program is relatively inexpensive and actually does the job that it promises to do.

As the *Philosophy For Young Thinkers Program* began to take shape, we gradually substituted philosophical problem-solving for future problem-solving. The methods and ideas developed by the Torrance Center have been kept and from time to time we have rewritten FPS problems in a more philosophical manner to add a more indepth conceptual dimension to the program.

The Renzulli Triad and the Paideia Proposal have much in common. Both emphasize exploring a variety of content, the development of higher level thinking and learning skills, and an enlarged understanding of ideas and values—Renzulli through research and Adler through the Socratic method and student participation. Because of its consistence with the other areas of the Tuttle AG Experience, the Renzulli Triad Model has become an effective administrative device for managing the program's varied dimensions.

Program Framework

The Tuttle AG Experience began with a set of clearly stated goals and objectives (see: Table #2). The following goal areas were given to the program because of their holistic nature and their innate flexibility:

Goal 1:   The teacher will recognize the importance of self-directed learning as a life-long goal for each student.

Goal 2:   The teacher will make a commitment to the development of the full potential of each student.

Goal 3:   The teacher will initiate training in problem-solving, creativity, and decision-making.

Goal 4:   The teacher will assist students with the development of higher level thinking skills and with oral and written communication.

Goal 5:   The teacher will encourage students to extend their motivation to achieve into all areas of the curriculum.

These goals appeared to us to be consistent with the fundamental philosophy of C. H. Tuttle Middle School: " . . . to educate the total child at his or her learning level and to provide for the gifted student at the level of his or her educational strengths, including creativity, critical thinking, and opportunities for interest exploration."

Consistent with this philosophy, the Paideia Proposal provided us with a general, liberal, and humanistic approach to teaching, rather than one which is specialized, vocational, and technical. The Paideia Proposal has helped us organize our teaching with regard to subject matter, skills and concepts. Also, it has provided a clear methodology for approaching each one of these areas of the curriculum. The Paideia framework is built around the concepts of "What," "Why," and "How."

What is to be learned falls under three categories:

(1)   Kinds of knowledge (at Tuttle Middle School, the AG program is built around a framework of high level reading in American literature).

(2)   Skills to be developed (in the Tuttle Middle School AG program, the skill areas include literature and reading skills, problem solving skills, critical thinking skills, and communication skills).

(3)   Understanding or insights to be achieved through the content and skill areas (in the Tuttle Middle School AG program philosophical concepts and problems have been added in order to enhance and enrich the literature program).

Why seeks a reason for learning these materials and skills. The reason in each case, as expressed in the Tuttle AG Experience goals and also in the Paideia Proposal, is the way the Tuttle AG Program serves the three objectives of basic schooling—

(1)   Earning a living;
(2)   Becoming a good citizen; and
(3)   Living a full and enriching life.

How we can help our students learn what is to be learned comprises three different methods of instruction:

(1)   Didactic teaching by lectures and textbooks;
(2)   Coaching in order to develop the basic habits through which all skills are possessed;
(3)   Socratic teaching by questioning and by conducting discussions of the answers elicited.

Stimulated by the Paideia Proposal and guided by the insights of Torrance and Renzulli, the AG program at Tuttle Middle School was organized to maximize the total educational environment of the student. The following program has been implemented consistent with the philosophy and goals of C. H. Tuttle Middle School curriculum as reflected in their self-evaluation statement of 1987.

The Tuttle AG Experience

COMPONENT ONE:

The first component of the Tuttle AG Experience is primarily *exploratory* in nature. It is our belief that the gifted middle school student needs both the time and the opportunity to explore a variety of topics without the normal pressures of grades and time limitations. At Tuttle, the exploratory emphasis of the gifted program includes, but is not limited to, the following activities:

(1) Resource persons, guest speakers, seminars;
(2) Career Day;
(3) Media presentations (plays, films, musical presentations, multi-visual programs);
(4) Field trips oriented to all phases of the curriculum, including science museums, historical sites and museums, literary and drama events;
(5) Learning activities designed by the teacher, including a science and history fair at different times during the year;
(6) Parent seminars. Six parent seminars are held during the year. Four of these feature guest speakers from the North Carolina Department of Public Instruction, Gifted Department; the North Carolina School of Math and Science; the North Carolina School of the Arts; and the North Carolina Governor's School Program.

COMPONENT TWO:

The second component of the Tuttle AG Experience involves the development of *higher level creative and critical thinking skills*. The Tuttle AG program emphasizes the following skills and reasoning processes:

Skills. . .
    Induction
    Deduction
    Concept Analysis
    Evaluation
Processes. . .
    Problem-solving
    Literary Analysis
    Moral Reasoning
    Logical Reasoning

Included with this *skills* emphasis are several enrichment programs in which student participation is encouraged: the North Carolina Math Counts

Competition, the Catawba County Soil and Water Conservation Speaking Competition, the North Carolina Literary Competition, regional science and history fairs.

Although not every gifted student will want to participate in each of these activities, most of Tuttle's AG students do participate in one or more of these programs. The goal is to provide as many outlets as possible for the students' creative and intellectual abilities.

Table #3 outlines the philosophical problem-solving methodology used with the Tuttle AG Program. Table #4 presents a typical philosophical-type unit and several lessons generated from this unit utilizing this methodology.

Table #5 presents a six week outline of reading lessons and philosophical problem-solving lessons in order to demonstrate the way these are used together in the Tuttle AG Program.

COMPONENT THREE:

Finally, the AG program at C. H. Tuttle Middle School encourages students to become involved in *independent research* in any subject area of particular interest and on topics which they wish to explore in more detail. The teachers in the Tuttle AG Experience stand ready to assist the student with projects undertaken for other teachers and to assist other teachers with the development of higher level academic activities for their classes.

Under Component Three the teachers in the AG program at Tuttle have begun the development of a literary magazine with their AG students. This magazine will be published three of four times during the school year and will require students to submit a variety of written material from poetry to short stories, essays, and interviews. The purpose of Component Three is motivation through exploration. It should be mentioned that all the components of the Tuttle AG Program focus on the student and the development of student abilities and sensitivities for a lifetime of productivity in American society.

CONCLUSION:

In 1981, the National Assessment of Educational Programs observed: "Schools are not developing in students adequate thinking skills or the ability to interpret what is read beyond a superficial level." In developing the Tuttle AG Experience, the purpose has been to meet the demands and challenges that contemporary society has placed on students. After all, the basis of a functioning democracy is an educated electorate which has both the desire and the ability to think for itself. The assumption that individuals can think for themselves without the proper training is belied by many examples from history, from the emergence of Hitler during the 1930's to the Jonestown massacre in more recent times.

The gifted program at C. H. Tuttle Middle School continues to seek out resources and individuals that can add to, expand and increase the educational success of its students. The teachers and administrators connected with gifted programs in the Catawba County School District continue to attend conferences, take graduate classes, and participate in workshops concerning gifted education. They subscribe to materials related to gifted curricula development and invite guest experts into the system to speak to teachers, parents, and students. We firmly believe that the best gifted program is the most flexible gifted program, open to the future and not bound by the past. We hope that this program and the many others with which we have been associated will continue to grow and mature.

Paideia Outline

Goal: Acquisition of Organized Knowledge

Means: Didactic Instruction Including Lectures and Responses/
               Textbooks and Other Aids in Literature and History

Areas of
Operations: AG Literature
(See: lesson plan outline, Table #5)

- -

Goal: Development of Intellectual Skills—Skills of Learning

Means: Coaching, Exercises, Supervised Practice

Areas of
Operation: Reading, Writing, Speaking, Listening, Problem-Solving,
               Exercising Critical Judgment
               (Philosophical Problem-Solving, Table #3)

- -

Goal: Enlarged Understanding of Ideas and Values

Means: Socratic Questioning and Active Participation

Areas of
Operation: Discussion of Books, Plays, Poetry, Future Problem-Solv-
               ing, Development of Philosophical Ideas and Concepts
Note: Both the 7th and 8th Grade AG classes will also be develop-
               ing a literary magazine in which the skills of writing, or-
               ganizing, and critical judgment will be practiced.

TABLE 1

Programs For The Gifted
Goals and Objectives

1.0 Goal	The Teacher Will Recognize the Importance of Self-Directed Learning As A Life-Long Goal For Each Student.
1.1 Objective	The teacher will encourage student persistence in the development of skills in order to enhance task commitment, responsibility for work being completed, and their involvement in the selection of projects and assignments.
1.2 Objective	The teacher will encourage out-of-school learning experience that will promote the full development of each student.
1.3 Objective	The teacher will assist students in evaluating their strengths and weaknesses and provide the resources and opportunities for their growth and understanding.
2.0 Goal	The Teacher Will Make A Commitment To The Development Of The Full Potential Of Each Student.
2.1 Objective	The teacher will recognize the individual qualities of each student and encourage the student to develop these unique talents and abilities.
2.2 Objective	The Teacher will develop lessons and activities that allow student input, enhance student self-esteem, and motivate students to excel in all areas of the curriculum.
2.3 Objective	The teacher will identify community and regional resources which can work to enhance students' interests and talents.
3.0 Goal	The Teacher Will Initiate Training In Problem-Solving, Creativity, and Decision-Making.
3.1 Objective	The teacher will give instruction in and provide opportunities for creative problem-solving and monitor the students' problem-solving techniques to determine progress.
3.2 Objective	The teacher will develop a classroom environment which is flexible and encourages creative risk-taking and divergent thinking.
3.3 Objective	The teacher will provide time for team activities that assist students in the development of inter-personal skills.
3.4 Objective	The teacher will provide time for the understanding of current social and political issues and encourage students to discuss, research, and debate alternative solutions to these conflicts.

4.0 Goal	The Teacher Will Assist Students With The Development Of Higher Level Thinking Skills And In Oral And Written Communication
4.1 Objective	The teacher will teach and encourage the use of such skills as analysis, synthesis, and evaluation during classroom activities.
4.2 Objective	The teacher will teach and encourage the use of logical consistency.
4.3 Objective	The teacher will provide opportunities for students to develop their oral and written communication skills.
5.0 Goal	The Teacher Will Encourage Students To Extend Their Motivation To Achieve Into All Areas Of The Curriculum.
5.1 Objective	The teacher will encourage students to master all assignments—in and outside of the AG program.
5.2 Objective	Incentives such as Beta Club, Honor Roll, and special classes will be provided to motivate the AG student to improve and achieve in all areas of the curriculum.
5.3 Objective	The teacher will help students recognize that learning is necessary for self-development, and, as such, is a goal in and of itself.
5.4 Objective	The teacher will write lesson plans and task descriptions based on the philosophy, goals, and objectives of this program.

TABLE 2

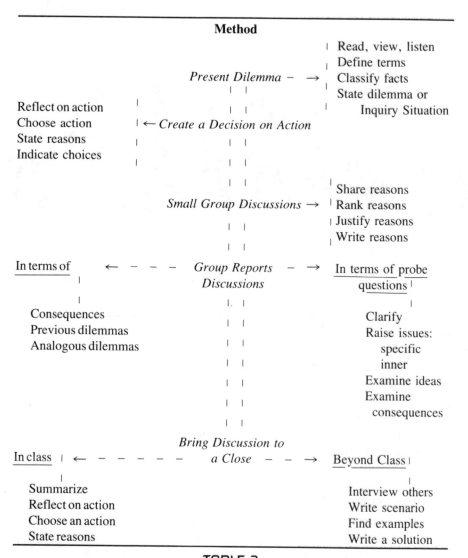

Method

Read, view, listen
Define terms
Present Dilemma – →   Classify facts
State dilemma or
Reflect on action   Inquiry Situation
Choose action   ← *Create a Decision on Action*
State reasons
Indicate choices

Share reasons
Small Group Discussions →   Rank reasons
Justify reasons
Write reasons

In terms of   ← – – –   *Group Reports*   – →   In terms of probe
Discussions   questions

Consequences   Clarify
Previous dilemmas   Raise issues:
Analogous dilemmas   specific
inner
Examine ideas
Examine
consequences

Bring Discussion to
In class   ← – – – – –   *a Close*   – – →   Beyond Class

Summarize   Interview others
Reflect on action   Write scenario
Choose an action   Find examples
State reasons   Write a solution

TABLE 3

Descent of Man

Skills:
  Inferring
  Looking for Assumptions
  Explaining

Concepts:
  Thinking
  Political Cartoon
  Viewpoint

Instructional Objectives:
  The student will. . .
  (1)   Understand the importance of thinking clearly and consistently.
  (2)   State the purpose and function of a political cartoon.
  (3)   Work cooperatively with other students in group discussions.

Procedures:
  The teacher will. . .
  (1)   Review with students the importance of thinking as a skill to be developed by all persons.
  (2)   Share with the class the objectives for this lesson.
  (3)   Engage students in the inquiry situation.
  (4)   Follow inquiry situation with activities, both oral and written.

Questions for Inquiry Clarification:
(1) What is the purpose of a political cartoon?
(2) How can critical thinking help individuals?
(3) What human problem does this cartoon address?
(4) Can you draw a cartoon as a position statement about some issue or problem in your life?
(5) Can you illustrate this point of view in another medium, such as music, poetry, short story, etc.?

Inquiry Situation: Independent Thinking

The political/social cartoon in this dilemma appeared in the *Charlotte Observer* on April 8, 1980. The purpose of a political cartoon is to express a point of view. In most major newspapers, cartoons such as this appear daily on editorial pages. They engage the visual imagery of readers in both "seeing" and thinking about the major issues of a society or nation.

Readers must interpret the message of these cartoons for themselves. Oftentimes, the cartoonist will have several messages tucked away in a suggestive visual or graphic presentation. When the particular point of view is recognized by readers, it can be a thought provoking experience. The cartoon's message is able to add meaning and significance to the reader's life situation.

Just how important is independent and critical thinking? In a free and open society such as America, democracy depends on people who not only can think for themselves, but who are given a free and unrestricted opportunity for independent thought to take place.

Critical thinking, concept analysis, and creative problem-solving will help people disseminate facts, make comparisons, discover hidden assumptions, identify implications, and evaluate solutions. Critical thinking involves analyzing data, ordering and interpreting information, and selecting relevant facts for application. An untapped reservoir of ideas, facts, opinions, and beliefs lies between your ears. To use the brain effectively, thinking should be directed toward solving important human problems; it should be purposeful.

Activity:

(1) Read the inquiry situation "Independent Thinking."
    A. Study the cartoon.
    B. What viewpoint is being expressed by this cartoon?

(2) Thoughtfully consider the cartoon.
    A. Give a title to this cartoon.
    B. What are your reasons for your title?
    C. Why do you think the author created this cartoon?

(3) Break up into groups of three students.
    A. Share your title, reasons, and opinions about the author's purpose with group members.
    B. Reach a group decision on each of these points of view.
    C. Justify and explain your reasons for your decisions.
    D. Write these reasons down in order of the most acceptable to the least acceptable.

(4) Each group will make a report (orally and written) to the whole class.
    A. Make sure the class understands each group's point of view.
    B. Let the class raise specific issues about the cartoon.
    C. Openly discuss and examine these ideas and their consequences.

(5) Bring the discussion to a close.
    A. In class. . .
    Summarize the major points that persons and groups have made about this cartoon.
        (1) Do you think the viewpoint in this cartoon focuses on a vital social issue? What is it?
        (2) Are there any hidden messages in this cartoon? What are they? Explain?
    B. Beyond class. . .
    Find examples from real life or printed material that illustrate the message of this cartoon. Share and explain.

DESCENT OF MAN
(Lesson Breakdown)

- -

Lesson One
Steps:

[1] Review with the students the importance of thinking as a skill to be developed by all persons.

[2] State objectives #1, #2, #3.

[3] Go over "Inquiry Situation." (present dilemma)

[4] Create a decision on action (Activities #1, #2).

[5] Small group discussion (Activity #3).

- -

- -

Lesson Two
Steps:

1. Review with students Lesson One.

2. State and review reason for this lesson.

3. Small group reports (Activity #4).

4. Bring discussion to a close (Activity #5,A).

- -

___

TABLE 4

Second Semester Lesson Plan Guide
The Tuttle AG Experience
1986-87

4th Grading Period

Materials:	*Cartoons for Thinking* *To Kill A Mockingbird* (8th Grade) *Roll of Thunder, Hear My Cry* (7th Grade)
Concepts:	Prejudice, Equality, Respect
Skills:	Induction, Deduction, Evaluation, Observation, Credibility of Assumptions, Finding Meaning

- -

Tuesday	The Descent of Man, Lesson One
Wednesday	Research of Depression era and assignment of novels to read: focus on prejudice
Thursday	The Descent of Man, Lesson Two
Friday	Workday for teachers

- -

Monday	Continue research
Tuesday	Living Together, Lesson One
Wednesday	Lesson: Life in the Thirties
Thursday	Living Together, Lesson Two
Friday	Living Together, Lesson Three

- -

Monday	Lesson continued: Life in the Thirties
Tuesday	Respect, Lesson One
Wednesday	Paper due/ Study of Key Characters
Thursday	Respect, Lesson Two
Friday	Test/Review

- -

Note:	On Monday and Wednesday of each week our classes are engaged in some phase of reading instruction via the use of stories, novels, etc. On Tuesday, Thursday, and Friday of each week our students are engaged in philosophical problem-solving related to their reading assignment. The purpose of the TTF emphasis is to reinforce the materials being read and allows work with students in skills development.

- -

Monday	Lesson, Symbolism, 8th grade
	Lesson, Point of View, 7th Grade
Tuesday	Human Equality, Lesson One
Wednesday	Lesson, Boo Radley Plot, 8th
	Lesson, Logan Family, 7th
Thursday	Human Equality, Lesson Two
Friday	Human Equality, Lesson Three

- -

Monday	Lesson, The Trial, 8th
	Lesson, Night Riders (KKK), 7th
Tuesday	Human Equality, Lesson Four
Wednesday	Lesson, the Trial, 8th
	Lesson, Man's Inhumanity to Man, 7th
Thursday	Human Equality, Lesson Five
Friday	Human Equality, Lesson Six

- -

Monday	Lesson, Man's Inhumanity to Man, 8th
	Lesson, Cassie Logan Grows Up, 7th
Tuesday	A Shattered Innocence, Lesson One
Wednesday	Lesson, Key Theme/paper due, 8th
	Movie for 7th and 8th grade
Thursday	A Shattered Innocence, Lesson Two
Friday	A Shattered Innocence, Lesson Three

- -

| Monday | Tests |
| Tuesday | Problem-Solving Evaluations |

TABLE 5

11 FACILITATING MORAL DEVELOPMENT

Before beginning a discussion on how to facilitate moral development, it is necessary to define and discuss Lawrence Kohlberg's theory of moral development. Kohlberg's work represents the seed from which additional studies of moral development have arisen. From his dissertation in 1958 to the present, Kohlberg and his disciples have refined and defined the theory of moral development. Without going into great detail, it seems clear to state that Kohlberg's theory draws heavily from the philosophical ideas of Plato, Kant, and Rawls with the addition of the psychological ideas of Dewey and Piaget. Fundamentally, Kohlberg expanded on Piaget's two stage theory of moral development. For Piaget, the ages 6-12 consisted of the heteronomy stage (rules laid down by adults with little questioning) and the autonomy stage (where rules are obeyed not because they are adult conceptions but because rules are important in group and society relations). Kohlberg replaced Piaget's two-stage theory with a six-stage theory of moral development.

KOHLBERG'S SIX-STAGE THEORY

1. Preconventional Level

At this level the child is responsive to cultural rules and labels of good and bad, right or wrong, but interprets these labels either in terms of the physical or the hedonistic consequences of action (punishment, reward, exchange of factors) or in terms of the physical power of those who enunciate the rules and labels. The level is divided into the following two stages:

Stage 1: The punishment-and-obedience orientation. The physical consequences of action determine its goodness or badness regardless of the human meaning or value of these consequences.

Stage 2: The instrumental-relativist orientation. Right action consists of that which instrumentally satisfies one's own needs and occasionally the needs of others.

2.   Conventional Level

At this level, maintaining the expectations of the individual's family, group, or nation is perceived as valuable in its own right, regardless of immediate and obvious consequences. The attitude is not only one of conformity to personal expectations and social order, but of loyalty to it, of actively maintaining, supporting, and justifying the order, and of identifying with persons or groups involved in it. At this level, there are the following two stages:

Stage 3: The interpersonal concordance or "good boy-nice girl" orientation. Good behavior is that which pleases or helps others and is approved by them.

Stage 4: The "law and order" orientation. There is orientation toward authority, fixed rules, and the maintenance of the social order.

3.   Postconventional, Autonomous, or Principled Level

At this level, there is a clear effort to define moral values and principles that have validity and application apart from the authority of the groups or persons holding these principles and apart from the individuals' own identification with these groups. This level again has two stages:

Stage 5: The social-contract legalistic orientation, generally with utilitarian overtones. Right action tends to be defined in terms of general individual rights, and standards that have been critically examined and agreed upon by the whole society.

Stage 6: The Universal-Ethical Principle Orientation. Right is defined by the decision of conscience in accord with self-chosen "ethical principles" appealing to logical comprehensiveness, universality, and consistency.

The stages exist in a hierarchy from the lowest level of moral development, punishment avoidance, to the highest stages of moral development which represents the Kantian Categorical Imperative: "Act only according to the maxim by which you can at the same time will that it should become a universal law." Lawrence Kohlberg's stage theory of moral development has the following characteristics:

(1)   Each of the stages imply an invariant sequence. Simply put, one does not skip stages but must progress from one stage to the next stage in a sequential, orderly manner.
(2)   The stages represent a total way of thinking. One does not use one method of thinking about one situation and another method on another situation. Thus the stages represent a total way of thinking.

(3)   Finally, the stage sequence is universal in nature. Each culture, regard-
      less of difference, reflects this sequence.

Following is an explanation and example of the various stages of moral
development:

Stage 1 centers on the use of punishment and obedience. One does an
action to avoid being punished. Young children may not understand the
rationale behind a particular request but they may understand the consequences for a particular action! For example, Bill was talking and playing
with his friend Jane. Bill wanted Jane to cross the road and play on the
other side. Jane told Bill that if she crossed the road to the other side, her
Dad would punish her since she had been told not to cross the road. Simply
put, she will not do the action in order to avoid the punishment. Thus, her
action is based on punishment avoidance.

Stage 2 is an attempt to establish and then seek actions which satisfy
one's own needs and occasionally the needs of others. An example of this
would be a child who needs a playmate in order to play house. The child
agrees to play with another child to have his/her needs met and perhaps
meet the needs of the playmate, i.e., Jane had been playing with her friend
Tom for several hours. She really didn't like Tom but he didn't know this.
The REAL reason she was playing with Tom was that she knew Tom's dad
would take her to the circus if she was around the house when he came
home. Thus Jane is more concerned with satisfying her own needs although
some of Tom's needs might be met.

Stage 3 reflects actions which please or help others and is approved by
them. This is very characteristic of individuals, i.e., adolescents who try to
meet the expectations and wishes of others in order to be accepted. The
"properness" of an action is determined by its acceptance within one's peer
group or family. As an example, Bob chooses to wear a particular type of
shirt because all his friends feel this is the "in" shirt. Or, Wanda decides
to attend the evening church service because of her parents' expectations.

Stage 4 represents an acknowledgment of the nature and importance of
laws and the maintenance of social order. At this point, the individual
follows laws because one should in order to maintain social order. The issue
of whether the law is moral is never considered. One simply does one's
"duty," not as a reflective thinker or one concerned with personal moral

choice, but because this is what one does in order to obey the laws and social norms of the society. When asked why she should obey a particular law, Jane replies, "I should obey this law because if everyone only obeyed laws they like, social order would break down. Laws are there to be obeyed."

Stage 5 features a social-contract legalistic orientation concerned with individual needs, as opposed to the social concerns of Stage 4. It many times has a utilitarian form of application in which majority or group rights are considered ahead of individual rights. The old dictum: "The greatest good for the greatest number" characterizes this stage. Individuals act in accordance with standards which have been agreed upon and critically analyzed by the whole of society. These standards are established in an attempt to provide the greatest good for the greatest number of people. Stage 5 attempts to develop minimal safeguards and rights for all people. Two excellent examples of Stage 5 application are the Constitution and the Bill of Rights. As an example, Jane now states that she will obey the law because the law maximizes the greatest good for the greatest number of people.

Stage 6 reflects an "universal-ethical principle orientation" which appeals to universality and consistency. John Rawls, in his book, *A Theory of Justice*, discusses principles of justice as those that would be chosen by rational persons acting in their own self-interest. This choice would occur within an initial position of equality. This also entails that ethical decisions be made by rational persons without knowing their possible socio-economic condition within life. This is also called the "veil of ignorance." In other words, I must decide what would constitute ethical actions without any consideration of my potential "place" in society. What would count as moral actions would be actions or laws which would not be concerned with socio-economic considerations or possibilities. Moral decisions are made based on principles, not possible outcomes. Developmentally, this type of moral decision-making rests at the peak of Kohlberg's hierarchy. There have been examples of individuals who initiated change based on Stage 6 reasoning. One of these individuals was Dr. Martin Luther King, who stated:

> One may well ask, 'How can you advocate breaking some laws and obeying others?' There are two types of laws, just and unjust. One has not only a legal but moral responsibility to obey just laws. One has a moral responsibility to disobey unjust laws. An unjust law is a human law not rooted in eternal and natural law. Any law that uplifts human personality is just, any law that degrades human personality is unjust.

For King, societal laws must be rooted in eternal and natural laws. This reflects both a religious and a philosophical (Kantian) influence. Kant did not base his categorical imperative on any experience to be verified but on an eternal principle that was before any consideration of application. It was within the idea of justice itself. It was part of its meaning.

In conclusion, if one compares the "Preconventional," "Conventional," and "Postconventional" levels of moral development, some critical differences begin to emerge. The preconventional level reflects egocentric interests. The conventional attitude reflects a consideration of the norms of the group (Stage 3) and the rules of the society (Stage 4). The postconventional reflects a consideration of ethical principles based on ideas and moral imperatives. Kohlberg, in a 1979 recording of data taken from moral judgment interviews, determined that 45% of 13-14-year-olds were reasoning at Stage 2, 42% at Stage 3, and 3% at Stage 4. Of the 16-18-year-olds, 20% were at Stage 2, 60% at Stage 3, and 14% at Stage 4. From these data one notes the movement from preconventional norms to conventional norms or from self-interest to awareness of group needs, and for the 14% of 16-18-year-olds, to inner directed thinking and recognition of the value of laws.

It is not the intention of this chapter to argue that higher stages of moral development are more desirable than the lower stages. This appears to be quite evident. The issue is, "If higher stages of moral development are better, then how can we as teachers facilitate this development?" What intervention strategies might be successful?

The authors of this book are assuming that if you are interested in the teaching of philosophy to students, then you are interested in helping students learn to think, analyze and evaluate various points of view. The following are some suggestions which should help individuals facilitate their moral development.

1.   The Classroom Should Represent An Effort To Implement Democratic Principles.

Students should be encouraged to participate freely in discussions within the class. The teacher or facilitator plays a critical role in these proceedings. The teacher should not attempt to indoctrinate his or her views on the students but instead, should attempt to educate. The goal of this program is educating for understanding. In the finest of the progressive tradition, the teacher should encourage each student to use his/her experiences and the experiences of others to assess continually ideas and maxims. In this sense, the teacher becomes a participant with the student in the learning process. Through this effort, students begin to see the complexity of issues and the various points of view. An excellent method to utilize is the construction of dilemmas.

2. Create Dilemmas Which Will Require Dialogue And Discussions Within The Class Environment.

The dilemmas presented within the book are only a beginning. Each discipline has issues which should engage students in dialogue and interpretation. The authors have worked across disciplines and taught many teachers how to write dilemmas, or as we prefer to call them, "Philosophical Problem Sheets" (PPS), for use in their class. There are several simple rules to follow.

(A). The teacher should attempt to recognize issues involving various points of view. For instance, literature is full of examples of free will vs. determinism. The teacher should attempt to write a "Philosophical Problem Sheet" (PPS) which illustrates this dilemma. The PPS should reflect various positions. For instance, perhaps one person would argue that we are free to do everything. Another might argue that human actions are determined. Another might argue for a combination of the two. What is of critical importance is to make sure the positions are clear and distinct and give students the opportunity to reason and decide.

(B). The teacher should attempt to introduce this concept before beginning the actual academic readings. This accomplishes several objectives. Students are made aware of an important issue which will arise in the reading. Secondly, they have discussed the dilemma issue and are therefore familiar with its tensions and problems. As an example, before having students read John Stuart Mill's work, *Utilitarianism*, I would introduce this concept to students with the use of PPS. The students would be better able to discuss this important work after having been made aware of the critical issues within the writing.

(C). Students should be encouraged to work independently and then in small groups. This accomplishes several objectives. 1) Students have time to independently reflect before sharing their ideas with others. Providing this reflection time will allow the student to evaluate competing alternatives. 2) After individual reflection, the students should work to evaluate the PPS in small groups. By working in small groups students are assured a chance to share their ideas with others. Of special importance for the teacher is the placing of students in groups which will maximize the participation of each student (see Table 3).

(D). The students should engage in class discussions. The students should feel free to point out various issues acknowledged within the groups or individually. The teacher must act as facilitator to keep the discussion moving in a consistent manner. Practice is the key to developing this skill. However, there are several points to keep in mind.

(1) Student input should be noted on the board for further reference. Generally, a few notes are all that is needed.

(2) The teacher must have an idea of the issues which will be covered during the discussion. This helps the students center on a particular idea.

(3) Discussions oftentimes will involve several days of classroom time. During Fall semester 1986, one of the authors taught a philosophy class in the public schools. The classroom was 80% discussion. In order for the students to be prepared for discussions, it was essential that they were prepared for class. Their preparation made the classroom atmosphere pleasant and yet demanding for both teacher and student.

(E). The teacher must add closure once the discussion is completed. This is essential. Closure allows for a review of the topic. In addition it can reinforce the questions which will need additional work and clarification. For students, this is a time to reflect on their work and ideas. In this manner the students can "see" what has been learned through their active involvement (see the sample lessons in Chapters 9 and 10).

Additional Considerations

There are several other considerations which could be used in the facilitation of moral development. An obvious issue is the importance of asking good questions. Jacob Bronowski in his excellent work, *The Ascent of Man,* remarks that Niels Bohr, one of the founders of quantum physics, used to begin his lecture courses by saying to his students, "Every sentence that I utter should be regarded by you not as an assertion but as a question." It is my feeling that this attitude is the key to the attainment of knowledge and wisdom. One must not rest upon accepted dogma but must think and analyze viewpoints and present this process to students. In order to teach, one must be willing to learn. The learning process demands that we ask questions, perhaps "silly" ones, in order to broaden our knowledge and understanding. If we as teachers are willing to question and evaluate assumptions, then our students will surely feel that they can do the same. A good question will oftentimes result in a good or novel answer.

If we can agree that asking a good question is important, then how do we become better questioners? The answer is not simple although perhaps there are some guidelines. The level of questions one is asking can be compared to Bloom's Taxonomy. One's questions should go from knowledge questions to questions which will involve analysis, synthesis and evaluation. This does not mean that a facilitator can make-up questions before class and simply use them during a discussion. Issues arise which will need your clarification and extension. In this manner you must conceive of questions while facilitating the discussion. Therefore before beginning a discussion, think of possible questions which may act as guidelines. Be sure these questions will require thinking rather than a simple response on the part of students.

Another tool is the use of a journal. A journal allows students time to reflect on readings and class discussions. Some students are quiet or rarely speak out in class. In a discussion oriented classroom, it might be hard to know what these students are thinking. While teaching philosophy in the public schools, one of the authors required all the students to keep journals. Their writings never ceased to provide enjoyment and satisfaction that these students were philosophers. Although taking a great deal of time, the author read and commented a great deal within the journals. At first the students were amazed that someone would take so much time to read their work. Afterwards, they continued to treat the journals with a great deal of importance and expected a thorough reading and comments on the part of the teacher! The students were able to use the journals to see how they were thinking about issues at the beginning of the class and how their thoughts evolved as the class proceeded. This was a source of great pride for both the student and teacher.

What has been presented is only a very brief and pragmatic summary of some ideas on fostering thinking and moral development for students. There is a great deal of additional information available for interested readers. The following books are highly recommended:

Brenda Munsey (Ed.) *Moral Development, Moral Education and Kohlberg.* 1980.
Ronald Duska and Mariellen Whelan. *Moral Development: A Guide to Piaget and Kohlberg.* 1975.

Both of these books provide excellent introductions to the philosophy and theory of moral development. Both books discuss the application of theories of moral development within religion and education. These are excellent works to see the various possible applications of moral theory.

Lawrence Kohlberg. (Vol 1) *The Philosophy of Moral Development*. 1981.
Lawrence Kohlberg. (Vol 2) *The Psychology of Moral Development*. 1984.

These two books are essential for the understanding of the stages of moral development from both a philosophical and psychological perspective. In addition, these works present a wonderful picture of the working of an insightful, creative mind.

James Rest. *Development in Judging Moral Issues*. 1979.
James Rest. *Moral Development: Advances in Research and Theory*. 1986.

Of particular interest is Rest's "Defining Issues Test" (DIT), which represents an objective measure of moral development. The DIT is discussed in length in the first book. The second book discusses new insights in the facilitation of moral education utilizing research and theory. Both books present excellent outlines of research studies which have attempted to facilitate moral development.

Norman A. Sprinthall and W. Andrew Collins. *Adolescent Psychology: A Developmental Approach*. 1984.

This book is essential to understanding how adolescents think and reason. The book provides a wonderful summary of the ideas of Piaget, Kohlberg and other major developmental theorists. This book is a must for your library!

CONCLUSION

There is a book, edited by Norman A. Sprinthall and Ralph L. Mosher, entitled, *Value Development . . . as the Aim of Education*. The authors find this title to be very special for we view the aim of education to be the facilitation of values development or moral development in individuals. Throughout the book, *Philosophy for Young Thinkers*, the authors have presented an outline, possible objectives and methods to meet these goals. It is now up to you, the reader, teacher, and learner. You must decide whether these purposes have validity within your students' educational needs and goals.

It is our hope that you will find these ideas and materials of some use. However, it is a far greater hope that you will develop materials of your own, within your subject area, to facilitate thinking and moral development among your students. Indeed, if properly presented, one cannot help but facilitate moral development simply by asking students not to memorize, but to think and reflect. Socrates stated, ''The unexamined life is not worth living.'' If this is so, we as educators have a moral obligation to help students examine this life, and the society in which it exists, in a supportive, caring environment. Truly, a democracy can only be strong if there are individuals who will participate and be heard. Our job as teachers is to ensure that the inquisitive minds necessary for a democracy continue to develop within our schools and community. We can make no greater contribution.

DEFINITION OF TERMS

A POSTERIORI
Knowledge which comes from experience.

A PRIORI
That which is known through reasoning, prior to experience.

AUTHORITARIANISM
The idea that the most valid source of knowledge comes from some kind of authority or belief.

AXIOLOGY
The study of values of all kinds.

BEHAVIORISM
The psycho-social theory which maintains that all knowledge of human behavior is based on an objective observation.

COGNITION
The act of knowing through sensory experience.

CONCEPT
The general idea of a class of objects.

CONTINGENT
That which can be equally well conceived as not existing; that which might be the case as contrasted with that which must be the case.

CONTRADICTION
A proposition which can be shown to be false by an examination of the symbols and logic of language.

DEDUCTION
The process of reasoning in which conclusions are drawn from accepted premises.

DETERMINISM
The theory that every event is totally conditioned by its cause or sequence of causes.

EGOISM
In the field of ethical theory, a doctrine which identifies the good with one's own pleasure or well being.

EMPIRICISM
The doctrine that the source of knowledge is experience and that all human knowledge is limited to the possible scope of human experience.

EPISTEMOLOGY
The area of philosophy which is interested in the nature, sources, and limitations of human knowledge.

ETHICS
The area of philosophy whose purpose is to clarify and validate a set of principles for human conduct.

ETHNOCENTRISM
The attitude that one's own way of life is the highest and best and by comparison, all other ways of life are secondary.

EXISTENTIALISM
The philosophical theory which views human nature as having no fixed patterns but as free and creative.

FATALISM
The idea that all events are determined by nonhuman causes.

HEDONISM
Within ethical theory, the idea that pleasure is the only intrinsic good.

HUMANISM
An idea usually associated, but not necessarily, with naturalistic or non-theistic doctrines; emphasizes human nature, growth, and development as opposed to the supernatural.

IDEALISM
A philosophy which reduces all existence to mind.

INDUCTION
Inference from observation of particular instances to general conclusions yielding probable knowledge.

MATERIALISM
The philosophical idea which says that the entire universe, including the human mind, can be explained in terms of matter in motion.

METAPHYSICS
The study of ultimate reality rather than just a part of nature.

NORMATIVE
That which pertains to any norm, principle, or standard of evaluation.

POSITIVISM
A philosophical theory which limits all knowledge to the scientifically verifiable.

PRAGMATISM
A view which emphasizes that meaning and truth depend upon consequences or results.

RATIONALISM
The view that knowledge is to be tested not by sensory methods, but by deduction and reason.

RELATIVISM
The thesis that truth is relative to time, place, and group; there is no absolute and final truth.

SKEPTICISM
The idea that certain or absolute knowledge cannot be attained by human beings.

THEISM
The doctrine that God exists.

VALIDITY

In logic, a conclusion which necessarily follows from accepted premises.

VERIFIABILITY

The possibility of a statement being confirmed or established as true or false by empirical methods.

BIBLIOGRAPHY

CONCEPTUAL SCHEME ONE:
EMERGING HUMANITY

Kahn, Theodore C. *An Introduction To Hominology: The Study of the Whole Man.* Springfield: Charles C. Thomas Publishers, 1972.

Klapp, Orrin E. *Models of Social Order.* Palo Alto: National Press Books, 1973.

Packard, Vance. *The People Shapers.* Boston: Little, Brown, & Company, 1978.

Samples, Bob. *The Metaphoric Mind.* Reading: Addison-Wesley Publishing Company, 1976.

Swanson, Carl P. *The Natural History of Man.* Englewood Cliffs: Prentice-Hall, 1973.

Westphal, Fred. *The Activity of Philosophy.* Englewood Cliffs: Prentice-Hall, 1969.

CONCEPTUAL SCHEME TWO:
THE SELF AND SELF-AWARENESS

Buber, Martin. *Between Man and Man.* New York: The MacMillan Company, 1968.

Burtt, E. A. *The Metaphysical Foundations of Modern Science.* Garden City: Doubleday, 1932.

Byrne, Edmund F. and Maziarz, Edward A. *Human Being and Being Human, Man's Philosophies of Man.* New York: Appleton-Century-Crofts, 1969.

Gardner, John. *Self-Renewal.* New York: Harper & Row, 1964.

Kostelanetz, Richard. *The Edge of Adaptation, Man and the Emerging Society.* Englewood Cliffs: Prentice-Hall, 1973.

Matson, Floyd W. *The Broken Image.* New York: Doubleday, 1964.

Stewart, E. W. and Glynn, James A. *Introduction To Sociology.* New York: McGraw Hill, Inc., 1974.

CONCEPTUAL SCHEME THREE: VALUES/MORAL THINKING

Baier, Kurt and Rescher, Nicholas. *Values and the Future*. New York: The MacMillan Company, 1969.

Benn, S. I. and Peters, R. S. *The Principles of Political Thought: Social Foundations of the Democratic State*. New York: The Free Press, 1959.

Bronowski, J. *Science and Human Values*. New York: Harper Torchbooks, 1965.

Fromm, Eric. *Man for Himself: An Inquiry into the Psychology of Ethics*. Greenwich: A Fawcett Premier Book, 1947.

Hudson, W. D. *Modern Moral Philosophy*. Garden City: Doubleday and Company, 1970.

Ross, David. *The Nature of Moral Responsibility*. Detroit: Wayne State University Press, 1973.

CONCEPTUAL SCHEME FOUR: KNOWLEDGE AND UNDERSTANDING

Beardsley, Elizabeth L. and Beardsley, Monroe C. *Invitation To Philosophical Thinking*. New York: Harcourt Brace Jovanovich, Inc., 1972.

Hall, James. *Knowledge, Belief amd Transcendence*. Boston: Houghton Mifflin Co., 1974.

Hill, Thomas English. *Contemporary Theories of Knowledge*. New York: The Ronald Press Company, 1961.

Kahane, Howard. *Logic and Contemporary Rhetoric*. Belmont: Wadsworth Publishing Company, Inc., 1971.

Organ, Troy Wilson. *The Art of Critical Thinking*. Boston: Houghton Mifflin Company, 1965.